Exile at Small-Time U

Exile at Small-Time U

*Essays from the Trenches
of Embattled Academia*

Edited by DOUGLAS HIGBEE

McFarland & Company, Inc., Publishers
Jefferson, North Carolina

ISBN (print) 978-1-4766-9572-3
ISBN (ebook) 978-1-4766-5564-2

LIBRARY OF CONGRESS CATALOGING DATA ARE AVAILABLE

Library of Congress Control Number 2025017622

© 2025 Douglas Higbee. All rights reserved

No part of this book may be reproduced or transmitted in any form or by any means, electronic or mechanical, including photocopying or recording, or by any information storage and retrieval system, without permission in writing from the publisher.

Front cover image: Adobe Firefly

Printed in the United States of America

*McFarland & Company, Inc., Publishers
Box 611, Jefferson, North Carolina 28640
www.mcfarlandpub.com*

To the next generation of humanities faculty

Acknowledgments

First and foremost, I thank the contributors to this collection for their hard work, candor, and faith in the project.

I thank the University of South Carolina, Aiken, for a sabbatical leave to complete work on this book, and my faculty colleagues there, notwithstanding some of our differences.

I thank my son, Henry, and daughter, Maisie, who make it all worth it.

Table of Contents

Acknowledgments — vi
Preface — 1
Introduction
    Douglas Higbee — 3

Part I: Beginnings

The Allegory of the Classroom: Platonic Ideals, Material Chaos, and My Initiation into the Regional Public University
    Chene Richard Heady — 15

"You are going to be fired, but I can't tell you why": Academic Politics in an Appalachian College
    Wayne Wisher Combs — 22

Exiled Before I Began
    Matthew Boedy — 32

Making the Most of the Rest of Your Career: Confessions of a Public Historian in Southwest Georgia
    Evan A. Kutzler — 38

Life on I-57: Place, Placelessness, and the Commuting Academic
    Camden Burd — 47

"Wherever You Go, There You Are": Finding Myself in Academia
    Elizabeth Tacke — 54

To the Fringes and Back: Academic Life in the Rural Midwest
    Camilo Peralta — 63

Becoming an Academic in Japan: Negotiating Age,
    Gender and Nationality
    SUZANNE KAMATA 70

Academic Freedom in Erdogan's Turkey
    EVREN ALTINKAS 80

Part II: The Long Run

Seeking Grace: University Faculty in a Post-Covid, Anti-CRT,
    Anti-DEI, Anti-Tenure Environment
    DEREK CHARLES CATSAM 89

A Chronicle of Exile
    DOUGLAS HIGBEE 97

At Your Service: Faculty Workload and Self-Advocacy
    ERIN B. JENSEN 109

From Professor to Comedian and Back Again: A Case
    Study of Infusing Academics with Comedy
    MATTHEW McKEAGUE 114

The Whole Truth, Nothing But: Learning to Teach
    at a Small Rural University
    LOUIS YOUNG 120

I Quit: When the Tenure Track Is a Dead End
    KATHRYN D. BLANCHARD 131

On Not Getting Tenure
    G. THOMAS COUSER 136

Teaching Writing in Prison
    NANCY MACK 143

Travels on the Prairie and Other Adventures in Academia
    EDITH BORCHARDT 152

The Not So Good Old Days? Happy in Hindsight
    EUGENE STELZIG 161

About the Contributors 171
Index 175

Preface

This book is about what it's like to be a professor in the humanities at non-elite universities and colleges.

This book is not a history of the American university. It's not about the chronic adjunct crisis, or about academic politics at research universities. It's not another "end of the university" book either. There are plenty of those already published. Nor is it scholarly in nature. There are very few sources cited and no bibliography at the end of the volume. It's not a how-to book, though we hope it is nonetheless useful.

This book serves two purposes. First, it provides a series of autobiographical snapshots from 19 full-time professors from around the United States (and two foreign institutions) of the changes occurring at regional state universities and poorly endowed public and private colleges in the last couple of decades. These changes are a historical phenomenon as much as they are personally and professionally impactful. Second, in providing a set of first-person perspectives on these changes, we hope readers will come to better understand the current state of the modern university, and that current graduate students in the humanities, and undergraduates contemplating graduate school, as well as their advisors, find this book particularly informative, if not bracing.

Introduction

Douglas Higbee

> Democracy cannot flourish where the chief influences in selecting subject matter of instruction are utilitarian ends narrowly conceived for the masses, and, for the higher education of the few, the traditions of a specialized cultivated class.
> —John Dewey

> Oh I used to be disgusted
> And now I try to be amused
> —Elvis Costello

Before delving into the essays themselves, I invite the reader to consider the following paragraphs (the only "scholarly" paragraphs in this book), which will provide some context for the experiences and views presented here by the contributors. My hope is that this introduction will reduce the likelihood that such experiences be interpreted as the product of merely personal, or idiosyncratic, tendencies, since they are in large part the result of historical trends that have reshaped much of what we know as "the academy."

Liberal Expansion, Conservative Retrenchment, and the 21st-Century University

The thirty-year period from World War II to the early 1970s saw a level of economic growth that is unique in U.S. history ("Post-World War II"). Not only did this period facilitate a major rise in home ownership and an enlarged social safety net, but the Servicemen's Readjustment Act of 1944 (also known as the GI Bill) led directly to huge increases in college enrollment. The number of college students grew from 350,000 in 1910 to 14 million in 1990, and the number of degree-granting institutions of higher education grew from 950 to over 3,500 by 1990 (Snyder 76–77, 75). Among that last number, as of 2023 over 500 regional comprehensive universities enrolled 57 percent of U.S. students seeking a bachelor's degree (Garcia). Most of these regional campuses grew from teachers' colleges after World War II or were built in the 1950s and '60s. Among the 19 contributors to this volume, 16 work at regional state universities or at universities that grew out of teachers' colleges after World War II. My own campus, the University of South Carolina, Aiken, is a regional comprehensive institution founded in 1960.

The liberal-era high tide eventually receded. In the wake of the Reagan Revolution, regressive tax policies and a rollback of government investment in social goods put downward pressure on the funding of public universities and hollowed out the concepts of public education and the public good itself. The 2008 recession, the worst financial crisis since the Great Depression, exacerbated these trends (O'Leary and Perez). At my own institution, for example, in 2002 approximately 50 percent of revenue came from state appropriation; in 2010, it was close to 10 percent (statistics supplied by USC Aiken budget director).

The starkest result of this conservative retrenchment is an ever-tightening academic job market, especially the marked increase in the percentage of faculty working as adjuncts, paid on a class-by-class basis with few to no benefits. According to the AAUP, 33 percent of faculty members in U.S. colleges and universities held full-time tenured or tenure-track appointments in 2021, compared with 53 percent in 1987 (Colby). But another long-term consequence of this retrenchment is the increasing dominance of quantitative assessments—often mandated by state legislatures—as a marker for academic quality. The emphasis on pass/fail and graduation rates, for instance, presumes that a college education is merely a means to an end, and even an obstacle to such ends, rather than valuable in itself. And when such measures become the benchmark for this or that academic program's value or relevance, those programs that are intellectually difficult—ones that require a certain level of writing skill or mathematical facility—are often targeted for downsizing by administrators. While Bill Readings counseled nearly 30 years ago that "university presidents [need to begin] thinking about questions of value [rather] than juggling indices of excellence and filling in charts of 'goal achievement'" (133), the use of quantitative assessments—and administrative reliance on them—has only increased. A related administrative technique is "strategic planning," a process that usually begins with the hiring of an expensive consulting firm, which gathers input from various campus "stakeholders" and then ends with the administration cherry-picking its preferred initiatives. As Benjamin Ginsburg, author of *Fall of the Faculty*, explains, such strategic plans "take enormous energy for no reason. Many of these could just be copied; the end result would be the same. The process of putting these plans together is designed rather like elections in the Soviet Union: the process is designed to give people the impression that people care what they think" (Berrett).

Perhaps the most onerous example of this assessment regime is the near-universal reliance on students to evaluate teaching. Though in principle not an entirely objectionable idea, in practice these end-of-term exercises are usually implemented as simplistic, multiple-choice surveys, which offer very little useful evidence for what actually happens in the classroom, especially with the humanities and liberal arts in general. Much of what happens in a humanities course in terms of learning is subtle, and often doesn't come to fruition until years after graduation. Quantitative assessments—and such corollaries as concrete "learning outcomes"—are especially unable to account for this kind of learning. But such assessments are cheap, much cheaper than an actual program, such as a robust, formative peer-observation system, that might help faculty keep their teaching skills sharp and up to date. Yet student evaluations, even when their response rates are well below 50 percent, as they often are, nonetheless are often used as one of the primary indicators of a professor's skills, and whether they merit promotion and tenure, or, as with annual review and post-tenure review (further retrenchment-era additions to faculty assessment), whether tenured faculty should be retained at all.

Increasingly, these assessment regimes have put the values and interests of liberal arts programs at odds with more vocational programs such as business, nursing, engineering, education, and so forth, particularly at regional comprehensives and non-elite private colleges. Academic programs that seem less "cost-effective," particularly those in the liberal arts, have seen further decreases in enrollments as administrators invest their dwindling resources into more vocational programs and cash-strapped parents feel unwilling to fund "impractical" degrees. In South Carolina, for instance, the state offers scholarships to students specifically for STEM majors ("LIFE and Palmetto Fellows"). Even though there is plenty of evidence available that humanities majors do as well financially as most of other majors over the long term, and that the skills learned in humanities programs are in demand by top companies, this disciplinary favoritism adds yet another stressor to the viability of humanities and liberal arts programs.

We see more evidence of this retrenchment in the reduction in liberal arts requirements in general education curricula and an acceleration in cuts to liberal arts programs. Just recently, for instance, my university removed the foreign language requirement and the upper-level writing assessment from the gen-ed curriculum. Probably by the time this book is published more cuts will have been made. Just recently the governor of South Carolina called for a state-wide evaluation of the academic necessity and economic viability of all colleges and universities. In states like Pennsylvania, such consolidations have already occurred, and several other states are considering such changes (Gardner, "More States"). West Virginia University recently "slashed 28 undergraduate majors and graduate programs, terminating 143 faculty (many of them tenured), and completely eliminating the study of foreign languages at WVU." According to the president of WVU, "academic programs exist to serve the 'future needs of industry.' Any form of study that does not translate directly to career outcomes is [...] irrelevant" (Pettit). The interested reader can search online for "general education revision" and "liberal arts program cuts" to find myriad other examples.

In response to the conservative weakening of public investment in higher education and the corresponding need for stable enrollments, many colleges and universities have looked to the internet as a lifeline. Moving classes online allows more students to enroll for relatively little increase in overhead. The Covid-19 pandemic only increased the use, and dependence upon, digital technologies. While online instruction might help with enrollment, classes which emphasize skills such as writing and critical thinking—the stock-in-trade of liberal arts programs—do not transfer as well to an exclusively online format. Further, online "classroom management systems" such as Blackboard make the intellectual property of professors more vulnerable to abuse, and new AI programs such as ChatGPT threaten to erode students' need to learn good writing themselves.

A Two-Tiered System

These developments have put serious pressure on the quality of university-level instruction, especially in the liberal arts. But the fact is elite institutions and flagship campuses of state universities have been relatively insulated from such financial and intellectual retrenchment, and thus are much more resistant to the kinds of systemic changes described above than institutions such as regional comprehensive universities and non-elite liberal arts colleges.

Take Harvard University, for example. Its endowment, the largest in the world, has grown from $4 billion in 1990 to approximately $50 billion, reflecting its deep investment in the stock market ("Harvard"). Most other elite private colleges and state university flagships have multi-billion-dollar endowments as well ("List of Colleges"). Conversely, the current endowment of my institution, USC Aiken, is $36 million ("University"). A professor at a branch campus of Colorado State University writes that "our university system spends almost three times more on student instruction at the flagship campus—$13,700 per student in Fort Collins versus $4,787 in Pueblo" (Eskew). Perhaps not every state university system's budgeting aligns with this example, but it is clear, in general, that flagship campuses and other institutions with large endowments have done much better than regional campuses in weathering the economic retrenchment of the last generation. In fact, according to the U.S. Department of Education statistics, "in 28 states, flagships have seen enrollment rise between 2010 to 2021, while regionals have trended down" (Gardner, "Flagships Prosper").

My point here is that this two-tiered system of funding—elite institutions buffered from socio-economic pressures via large endowments vs. the financial vulnerability of regional state universities and non-elite private college—has created a significant gap in what sort of education these institutions are able to offer, respectively. Schools vulnerable to financial and enrollment pressures offer less and less of what most of us would recognize as a liberal arts education.

Another recent example comes from the State University of New York system, currently in the process of reducing its humanities programs, particularly on its regional comprehensive campuses. As David Curry writes, "It is the 13 traditional four-year 'comprehensive' or liberal-arts colleges that are under attack. As just one indicator, three comprehensive SUNY campuses—Potsdam, Fredonia, and Plattsburgh—all of which had flourishing philosophy programs 10 years ago, have discontinued the major and now employ one full-time philosopher each."

Financial pressures have also left many regional schools more vulnerable to legislative interference. Whether that interference focuses on "free speech," mandated courses, CRT-related curricula, and so forth, public institutions are more often the target: "Reliance on public funding renders colleges increasingly vulnerable to legislative overreach, and thus to restrictions on academic freedom. As a result, public institutions are less protected than their private peers when it comes to research and teaching, despite benefiting from more robust First Amendment protections" (Ben-Porath and Bogia). And within the public education sector, regional campuses are the most vulnerable: "Those most vulnerable to conservative state-level leadership are all the public institutions that are not 'flagship' research universities" (Levenstein and Mittelstadt).

In my state of South Carolina, the legislature recently mandated a three-credit course in the university general education curriculum that requires "the reading of the U.S. Constitution, the Declaration of Independence, the Emancipation Proclamation, five Federalist Papers, and one document foundational to the African American Struggle; hereinafter collectively known as the "Founding Documents" ("REACH Act"). While there is nothing specifically objectionable about these texts, such a specific set of guidelines restricts the academic freedom of university faculties (especially history professors, in this case) to create courses based on the development of their own discipline, and, in an era when most institutions are reducing their general education requirements, squeezes out other essential offerings, such as writing or foreign language instruction.

In addition, several state legislatures have recently considered bills to eliminate tenure. Every one of these states is led by Republicans. My own district's state representative recently introduced a bill to end tenure in South Carolina ("Bill 4522"). Though none of these bills—aimed at all levels of public higher education, not just regional comprehensives—have become law, the continual threat makes the end of tenure much more likely. But perhaps a more urgent threat to tenure stems from the issues just discussed above—non-renewal of tenure-track faculty lines, and especially reductions and even elimination of liberal arts programs. In this climate, tenure—as well as the work liberal arts faculty actually do—has become less and less meaningful.

The Essays

In such circumstances, it should come as no surprise that liberal arts faculty—especially those at non–R1 institutions located in red or purple states—have found their professional identities more precarious and their work less satisfying. But because tenure-track jobs in the humanities are so hard to come by, we are often told to be grateful and to be quiet. Indeed, there is much to be grateful for. But there are still compelling, and necessary, stories to be told.

Yet relatively little autobiographical writing has been published about the subtle but life-changing personal and professional vicissitudes of a career working in a besieged field like the humanities in the academic trenches of branch state campuses and non-elite private colleges. There is some fiction, and plenty of sociological work, available on the subject, but very little personal or narrative nonfiction. James Lang's *Life on the Tenure Track* was published twenty years ago, before the Great Recession, the iPhone, and Covid-19. There are also plenty of books lamenting the present state of academe in general, but these texts lack the personal perspective that is the focus of this volume. And there are plenty of "how-to" guides for graduate students or graduate school administrators but texts such as these, while often helpful, are quite broad and aren't written from the first-person perspective. And while readers may have come across the occasional autobiographical piece in higher education journalism, the hope here is that a collection of essays will make a more comprehensive impact on our understanding of exile—of what it is like to work currently at baccalaureate-focused institutions under severe financial pressures, often far away from home and family. We have tried to tell it like it is, warts and all. A few essays have been written under a pseudonym, to protect their authors from possible retaliation.

The collection's essays are grouped into two categories, based on the chronology of a full-time academic career: life before and after tenure. The essays in Part I: Beginnings deal with life on the tenure track. Taken together, they present the challenges of building one's professional identity while suddenly finding yourself in a strange place, such as a rural small town, and a strange institution, negotiating the unwritten rules for new faculty in the era of neo-liberal university management. How do I survive? Do I stay or leave? Do I even have the option to stay?

The first several essays focus on survival. Chene Richard Heady wryly recounts his first year as a tenure-track English professor at a regional public university in rural Virginia, including getting caught up in petty departmental politics and running afoul of the department chair. Wayne Wisher Combs (a pseudonym) describes the first three years at his first tenure-track job as a religious studies professor at a rural community college in Appalachia, where he had to fend off the vengeful spouse of another finalist for his current position, an unpredictable college president, and community resistance to his teaching religion/Christianity in a scholarly manner. Matthew Boedy details his personal sense of exile in three ways: personal, as he almost got fired the first week on the job; disciplinary, in terms of the precarious position of rhetoric within English departments; and institutional, in terms of the increasingly precarious position of English departments within regional universities. Evan A. Kutzler's touchy meeting with former president Jimmy Carter, a local school board member in the 1950s, symbolizes the difficulties—and opportunities—of doing public history at a small, regional school.

The next few essays focus on exile in terms of location—especially negotiating the geographic and often emotional distance between the hard-won tenure-track position and powerful family and hometown ties. Camden Burd writes about his weekly commute between home in Chicago and his professorship in mid-state Illinois. For Burd, the freeway is not merely a conduit between places, but a place in itself, one which forces him to take stock of his academic identity. Elizabeth Tacke's piece drills down into the ennui of finding yourself, after the joy of landing a tenure-track position has dissipated, in a small, remote town in the Midwest, far apart from friends and family. Camilo Peralta humorously describes his academic odyssey from working as an adjunct and then non-tenure track instructor at rural colleges in Oklahoma and Kansas to his recent tenure-track appointment back home in Chicago.

The final two essays in Part I offer cautionary experiences from teaching overseas. Suzanne Kamata describes her search for a full-time professorship in Japan. Though she is ultimately successful, her essay offers important caveats for those considering teaching abroad. Evren Altinkas—quite literally an exile—was forced to resign from his university post at Artvin Coruh University because of support for the Gezi Park protests of 2013, a broad-based movement against Turkey's authoritarian regime. His essay offers food for thought for U.S. academics increasingly under attack by right-wing conservatives.

Part II: The Long Run focuses on what happens after tenure, from the middle years of one's career into retirement. Once the stresses of the tenure-track are completed, with several years of experience under one's belt, and the realities of one's job and the deeper wellsprings of one's institutional climate have become clear, what then? Just as with Part I, a variety of experiences are offered here.

Derek Charles Catsam examines the post–Covid-era pressures on faculty teaching in the liberal arts at a regional comprehensive university in terms of the gradually disappearing model of shared governance. I offer a diary-like series of incidents, found on the hard-drive of a recently absconded colleague, of a devoted humanist vacillating between idealism and cynicism. Erin B. Jensen emphasizes the difficulties in striking a healthy work-life balance, first at a small regional university and then at a small private college. Teaching several courses a semester and taking on numerous service tasks, Jensen looks for the right time to say "no." Matthew McKeague finds his first tenure-track job less than satisfying, and leaves to pursue a career in standup comedy in Los Angeles; after a couple years he obtains another tenure-track position, this time with a renewed sense of professional purpose and teaching assignments that make use of his California sojourn. Louis Young (a pseudonym) takes the reader through his personal and professional reinvention, the emotional and pedagogical process of coming to terms with teaching at a university in which many students are underprepared and beset by economic and social pressures that make academic success particularly difficult.

The last group of contributors look back on their academic careers. Kathryn D. Blanchard narrates the painful transition from idealism to disappointment in the years between landing a tenure-track position at a small private college and quitting as a full professor with an endowed chair. From the opposite perspective, G. Thomas Couser's essay offers a bracingly honest response to being denied tenure at his first academic position, and how he survived. Nancy Mack recalls her years teaching writing in male prisons in Ohio in the 1970s and '80s, a kind of exile from the "normal" academic life but one which, through trial and error, Mack found rewarding. Edith Borchardt's essay focuses on the balance she eventually struck between the difficulties of geographic isolation and the joys of engaging with students over a long career teaching at a branch campus of the University of Minnesota. Lastly, Eugene Stelzig provides some historical perspective. Even in the "good old days" before the recent downturn in the humanities job market, and even with a Harvard Ph.D., he received only one tenure-track offer, from a state college in rural New York. He describes getting used to the heavy teaching load, and frictions between the English department and the campus administration, but emphasizes the benefits of having the opportunity to teach what he loves.

Works Cited

Ben-Porath, Sigal, and Megan Bogia. "Academic Freedom Shouldn't Be a Privilege of Wealth." April 13, 2023. *The Chronicle of Higher Education.* www.chronicle.com.

Berrett, Dan. "The Fall of the Faculty." *Inside Higher Ed.* July 13, 2011. www.insidehighered.com.

"Bill 4522: Cancelling Professor Tenure Act." 2021–22. *South Carolina State Legislature.* www.scstatehouse.gov.

Colby, Glenn. "Data Snapshot: Tenure and Contingency in US Higher Education." *AAUP,* Spring 2023. www.aaup.org.

Curry, David C. K. "The Gutting of the Liberal Arts." April 8, 2024. *The Chronicle of Higher Education.* www.chronicle.com.

Dewey, John. *Democracy and Education.* Macmillan, 1916.

Eskew, Doug. "Regional Comprehensive Universities: Separate and Unequal." *Inside Higher Ed.* Aug. 1, 2023. www.insidehighered.com.

Garcia, Mildred. "The Community Focus with Regional Colleges." *The Evolution: A Modern Campus Illumination.* Sept. 12, 2023. www.evolllution.com.

Gardner, Lee. "Flagships Prosper, While Regionals Suffer." Feb. 13, 2023. *The Chronicle of Higher Education.* www.chronicle.com.

———. "More States Are Looking at Consolidating Their Public Colleges. Does It Work?" *The Chronicle of Higher Education.* July 30, 2020. www.chronicle.com.

"Harvard University Endowment." *Wikipedia.* www.wikipedia.com. Accessed March 23, 2024.

Levenstein, Lisa, and Jennifer Mittelstadt. "The Real Fight for Academic Freedom." Oct. 7, 2022. *The Chronicle of Higher Education,* www.chronicle.com.

"LIFE and Palmetto Fellows Math and Science Scholarship Enhancement." *South Carolina Commission on Higher Education.* www.che.sc.gov.

"List of colleges and universities in the United States by endowment." *Wikipedia.* www.wikipedia.com. Accessed March 23, 2024.

O'Leary, Brian, and Nick Perez. "State Support for Public Colleges, 2002–21." *The Chronicle of Higher Education,* Nov. 10, 2023. www.chronicle.com.

Pettit, Emma. "Gordon Gee's Last Stand." March 1, 2024. *The Chronicle of Higher Education*, www.chronicle.com.
"Post–World War II Economic Expansion." *Wikipedia*. www.wikipedia.com. Accessed March 23, 2024.
"REACH Act Guidelines." Dec. 2021. *South Carolina Commission on Higher Education*. www.che-dev.sc.gov.
Readings, Bill. *The University in Ruins*. Harvard UP, 1996.
Snyder, Thomas D., editor. "120 Years of American Education: A Statistical Portrait." Jan. 1993. *National Center for Educational Statistics*. https://nces.ed.gov/pubs93/93442.pdf.
"University of South Carolina Aiken." *DATAUSA*. datausa.io/profile/university/university-of-south-carolina-aiken.

Part I
Beginnings

The Allegory of the Classroom
Platonic Ideals, Material Chaos, and My Initiation into the Regional Public University

Chene Richard Heady

I hesitated at the door and peered inside the interview room at the Modern Language Association's annual convention. It looked like a giant high school cafeteria. In the middle of the room stood hundreds upon hundreds of collapsible tables, at each of which a tight group conversed with energy and enthusiasm, ignoring the rest of the world. Around the perimeter of the room, a herd of job candidates drifted anxiously, stopping every now and again to crane and squint. They looked for all the world like students new to a school, seeking with fear and self-loathing to find a lunch table that would somehow welcome them. The sight was grim enough that I turned back to the corridor.

Just outside the door, nervous job candidates sought reassurance from their parents on their flip phones or Blackberries. One exception: the overachiever who had actually brought his father along in the flesh. The overachiever accepted a paternal hug and drank in a stream of motivational clichés delivered in a South Boston accent, placed his suddenly inert parent just outside the door like a checked bag, and then strode with determination into the room. In the middle of the hotel hallway, one woman sat on the floor in the lotus position, eyes closed, rap music blaring from her earbuds. She suddenly jumped up, shouted, "Game face on!" and then charged into the interview room, oblivious of those she had nearly bowled over.

Since the hallway outside the interview room seemed an even more miserable place to be than the interview room itself, I entered behind her and drifted until I located the right collapsible table. Here as I leaned forward and nodded in what I hoped was an agreeable manner, I was told tales of a Southern college—let's call it Johnston State University—with a harmonious, dedicated, and student-centered faculty. A college that combined the affordability and access of a public institution with the small size and liberal arts emphasis of a private. A bucolic idyll. The place sounded like the product of another era, a time capsule from the 1930s. But the large metal eyeglasses and double-breasted suits of the interview committee also seemed to belong to another era, so I supposed it was possible, and anyhow what did a Michigander like me know about the South? I wondered whether someone like me—a first-generation college student who had paid his own way through a commuter college—really belonged at this sort of mossy, vine-covered institution. But Johnston State offered health insurance and a state pension and I determined that that was belonging enough for me. When the offer came, I took it.

Before my first term even began, the two central members of my search committee extended Southern hospitality by separately buying me lunch. An elderly Victorianist with a comb-over, big glasses, full beard, and a nervous grin treated me to a slightly upscale home style lunch in a converted nineteenth-century tobacco warehouse. I asked him how the steak was, and he told me he was a vegetarian. After my misstep, he took over the conversation. He gently rained small talk upon me until I was soaked. Polite questions about my move, my wife and her academic job, the town an hour away in which we were now living, and our dog slowly morphed into equally polite work-related complaints and pieces of advice: 1. It was good that I was so devoted to my primary area of specialization. 2. I shouldn't let anyone, however well-intended, distract me from my primary area of specialization. 3. Some faculty who weren't also Britishists might not be able to appreciate fully what I had to offer, but he certainly did. 4. He looked forward to working with me and the other literature faculty to keep the college's proud liberal arts tradition vibrant and alive in these changing times.

Only gradually did I begin to notice a reoccurring theme, even an implied narrative, hidden among the platitudes and pleasantries, a kind of backwards-masked message playing beneath the "Spring Rain" setting on a white noise machine. But I got the message pretty clearly. I heard: "I am the faculty member responsible for your hire. The others underrated you and worked against you. I expect your reciprocal loyalty in all departmental and university policy matters."

He rose to his feet, tilted his head to the side, said, "Onward," and walked out the door.

My next lunch was at a campus-area dive bar with a fortysomething bohemian creative writer whose long hair and peasant skirts were both wild and untamed. She had been on my search committee but hadn't been part of the MLA interview group. The first part of our conversation was a replay of the lunch I had had a few days before: I asked her how the hamburgers were and she told me she was a vegetarian. After my junior faculty misstep, the senior faculty member took over. In a manic torrent of words, interrupted only by the occasional smoker's cough or a raspy chuckle at her own jokes, she told me that it was amazing that working-class kids like us had been able to break into the Ivory Tower and that we had to stick together. The other members of the search committee would have overlooked my c.v. in the pile but she had immediately noticed my secondary specialization in creative writing. Creative writing was the future of the department and they needed another creative writer more than anyone knew. She didn't want to have to even get into all the dog fighting she'd had to do to get me here, but I didn't have to worry. She had my back. She bent over to light another cigarette, straightened and stood up, lifted the cigarette over her head as a parting benediction, and left without turning around.

So the image of a harmonious faculty vanished before day one of my first semester. I figured that the dueling conspiratorial narratives I had heard concealed a much more mundane truth: I was a compromise candidate whom neither committee member particularly wanted but whom both found acceptable. They had schemed against each other, the schemes had canceled each other out, and the result was me. This was, I later discovered, a more or less accurate impression. I resolved to keep my head down when it came to departmental politics and not to feel particularly obligated to anybody.

Since I had been told that I was now teaching at a hardcore liberal arts college, I had constructed my English syllabi around direct engagement with classic works. In Freshman Composition, I assigned Plato, Machiavelli, John Henry Newman, and Jean-Paul Sartre. In my general education British Literature survey, I assigned everything from Malory's *Morte d'Arthur* to T.S. Eliot's *The Waste Land*. Whether to avoid puncturing my illusions or to maintain their own (or perhaps maybe out of sheer indifference), no faculty member cautioned me against this move.

My misguided impression of the school didn't last long. One day in late August I gravely explained Plato's Allegory of the Cave, and then asked the class whether for Plato truth could be more reliably known through the senses or through the intellect. A guy with a short surfer haircut and stubbly beard, naturally seated at the back of the room, shouted, "Heart! The truth is in your heart, man!" And soon the rest of the class had joined him, enthusiastically proclaiming, through anecdotes rather than arguments, their allegiance to emotive and intuitive thinking, following the rabbit trail of the heart until they were lost deep in the woods, and I with them.

The class learned nothing that day, but I learned that the college that had been described to me at the MLA Convention and that at which I now taught were more incongruous than Plato's forms and material reality. Although the college was in fact old and rather pretty, the rest of the liberal arts bit was wishful thinking or some kind of strange Southern nostalgia. The college was your standard unselective public university early in the new millennium: few students did the reading and class discussion was apt to devolve into a series of graphic sex jokes, sometimes assisted with visual props (for instance, a female student turned a giant dry erase marker into a phallus, putatively to make a point about Freud). I soon had to compose an explicit policy against rolling joints in class ("Not in front of me, okay? If you're not worried about law enforcement, try to work on your time management, anyway"). I imagined that at least the small group of students who were perpetually pulling out pocket-sized red notebooks and jotting things down were taking class notes. I learned better at the end of the semester, when they presented me with the fruits of their labors: a typed list of the bizarre behaviors they imagined I would perform if I were drunk followed by a list of the odd occupations they hypothesized I must previously have performed (self-immolating chef, allergic perfume designer, phlegmatic fire-eater). A third, more factual, list, which itemized each time I had blushed at the class's graphic sexual references, was added as an appendix.

It didn't help my ethos that I was so exhausted from driving an hour each way to work and prepping up new classes for my 4/4 teaching load that I became weak in my grip and unsteady on my feet. I gesticulate whenever I make a point, and I watched helplessly as the dry erase markers I had been using escaped my feeble grasp, and flew off to whack unsuspecting students in the head. I pace when I talk, and I found myself frequently crashing into the instructional technology station, the podium, and the old-fashioned, wall-mounted pencil sharpener. I even fell down a flight of stairs in the English and Modern Languages building, jumping up and bowing to students once I hit bottom. The performance was, unfortunately, repeated.

At the December departmental holiday party, I discovered that even the seeming prevalence of vegetarianism among the Johnston State faculty was an illusion. The bearded Victorianist actually ate fish (and thus was more properly a pescatarian), while the chain-smoking creative writer abstained from all meat except for pork barbeque (an ethical position which has, understandably, no name). Like the college's identification as a "liberal arts university," their self-designation as "vegetarians" was just a linguistic performance for purposes of branding. As the party wound down, each cornered me for a private conversation. The Victorianist admonished me on ethical grounds against speaking too frequently to the Creative Writer: if the students saw me conversing with a chain smoker outside the English building, it might normalize smoking in their minds, leading them to become smokers, and eventually to get lung cancer. The Creative Writer more bluntly expressed her disappointment that I was already selling out my working-class roots by "playing it safe" and "class passing." She warned me that I didn't watch myself, I would become the Victorianist's next "mini-me."

As students jeered and faculty schemed, my department chair—a short man in blazer and tie with a haircut that made him look like a lost member of the Monkees—still resolutely conducted himself as if he were teaching at the college that had been described in my job interview. He lectured classes in the style of the knowing sage, locked the door on latecomers the second class started, and flunked any paper that contained more than three grammatical errors (greatly reducing his grading load in the process). Since he taught largely the same courses I did, it was no compliment to me that my classes were all full. When he went over my grade distributions and student evaluations, he contemptuously told me any positive evaluations I had received were the results of my insufficiently rigorous grading. He informed me that I had no business teaching post-modernism in a Twentieth Century Literature survey, since Great Literature had ended with D.H. Lawrence and Dylan Thomas. He interrupted one-on-one conferences with students to inform both me and the student what each of us should have been saying. To be fair, this was consistent with his own methods: it seemed that whenever I passed his office, I could see a different young blond woman leaning forward, carefully widening her eyes and earnestly nodding her head, as from somewhere beyond my line of sight he held forth.

My difficulties with the chair came to a head one day in Spring semester when I had finally tossed one dry erase marker too many and had to make a run to the departmental supply closet. Our supply closet was located in a first-floor hallway, unattached to any classroom; both the lock and lights could be accessed only from the outside. On my way there, I dropped by the department office and got the keys from the admin, which (as I later realized) allowed the chair to overhear my banal plans. I had stepped inside the supply closet and was reaching far back into the steel shelving unit for a box of dry erase markers, when the door shut behind me and the room went black. All was silent except for the snickering just outside the door. I sighed sadly because I immediately knew what must have happened: my department chair had turned off the lights and locked me in the supply closet. He thought this was a hilarious prank and retold the story at every possible occasion for the rest of the year. I began applying for jobs elsewhere.

The year closed with the buildup to a dramatic impeachment vote on the department chair (first came chair evaluations; then, a public meeting to advise the Dean; last, a formal vote). The Creative Writer signaled that I was to work against the department chair and the Victorianist signaled that I was to defend him, but neither bothered to say why. Then, just before I was about to turn into bed on a late-semester night, my home phone rang. It was the chair of the Promotion and Tenure committee calling to ask me why I had not filed my anonymous chair evaluation. Exhausted and irritated, I informed him I had not filed the evaluation because I had suspected that "anonymity" was a meaningless word at Johnston State, and that his phone call had not exactly dispelled my suspicions. In the public meeting that preceded the vote, the chair's defenders and detractors all agreed that the specific charges warranting impeachment would not be uttered. His enemies were too angry to repeat them and his allies wished to spare his good name. Consequently, in my first significant vote as a faculty member, I had no idea what I was voting about. I voted for impeachment anyway.

But if I had spent my first year discovering that the vision of the college with which I had been presented had been an illusion, I had at the same time been discovering that the students by contrast were real people. They were largely first-generation college students. Many of them experienced their attendance at an unselective regional public university less as a conscious decision than as the inevitable consequence of fate: they had been rejected from their dream school and had had to resort to a backup; or, parental preferences or economic circumstances had confined them to the college closest to home; or, having delayed college applications until the summer after high school out of procrastination or anxiety-induced avoidance, they had had to slip into whichever Ivory Tower still had a "Vacancy" sign lit up by the Admissions door. These were stories I understood. These students had once been my commuter college classmates, each with a story of what had gone wrong to bring them there, and each struggling forward towards something better. If they nodded right along with our soon-to-be-former department chair when he played the sage, it wasn't *just* because they knew that flattering teachers has always been a reliable path to a good grade; it was also because they didn't really believe they were actually capable of learning anything complicated. The day we had spent in Plato's cave had been paradigmatic: these students didn't sufficiently trust their minds as yet, but they really did have heart.

By the time I came to understand the students, however, I was chained to the textbooks I had already ordered, so I faced a pedagogical problem: my course content was essentially inalterable. Whether they liked it or not, my students were going to have to encounter complicated ideas as expressed in primary texts written by major thinkers. The only open question was what route we were going to take to our destination. Mostly because I couldn't come up with any other ideas, I gambled that we could zig-zag our way to intellectual summits if we approached our high-brow titles via low-brow methods. To explain Sartre's "Existentialism is a Humanism," I passed out a handout of quotations from *Batman Begins* (after all, as Batman says, "It's not who I am underneath, but what I do that defines me"; he's in all black; he could have worn a beret). Rather than ponderously explaining *The Waste Land* to the students and reducing the poem to a collection of footnotes, I broke the poem into fragments and the class into groups, gave each group a fragment, and told them that they were going to explain the poem to me. And when the time came, they were pleasantly surprised to find that they could do it. When I discovered that the students had been keeping a tally of how many times in my pacing about the room I stumbled or crashed into a piece of furniture, I encouraged them to take the logical next step and turn the tally into a betting pool.

Soon I found that these students were more willing to explore an idea, toss it around, and find a real delight in making sense of it, than those I had taught at larger and better-known universities. And they all stayed awake in class, if only to keep track of their odds of winning the betting pool. At the end of the semester, one of my students wrote in her course evaluation that although she couldn't imagine what I had done that made me deserve "to be sentenced to Johnston State," she was glad that she and her classmates were serving their time alongside me. So I shrugged my shoulders at the many absurdities around me and decided that, at least for now, I would stay on at the college; if I liked the students, I would deal with working on what essentially seemed to be a sitcom set.

"You are going to be fired, but I can't tell you why"

Academic Politics in an Appalachian College

WAYNE WISHER COMBS

All events described in this essay actually occurred, and the names are pseudonyms employed to shield the identity of all involved. For as much as academics like to project an image of being intellectuals with lofty ideals who hold socially important jobs like mentoring future generations, the brutal fact is that college faculty, staff, and administrators are just regular people. They argue, hold grudges, swear out restraining orders (this happened at a different college at which I worked), and sue each other.

Imposing Order on McGillicuddy College

My academic career at McGillicuddy College began when I was hired instead of someone who was "guaranteed" the position by an administrator. Of course, I did not learn this until after my hire. In my job interview, one of the four faculty members scarcely looked at me, which made me feel uncomfortable. This person asked the required questions but appeared completely disinterested in my answers. I felt better when Thom, the dean of the division, was brought into the interview and showed great interest in me.

Matters quickly got strange after I had been hired as Assistant Professor of History and Religion. It would take me until the beginning of the second week of Fall classes to arrive, because I was in the process of moving 3,000 miles to take the position. Just before I left, Thom informed me that an adjunct, the one who had been promised the job for which I had been hired, quit in the middle of a class. He simply made an announcement and walked out. When I arrived at the beginning of week two, I had to pick up that adjunct's classes as well as mine and encountered some confused students.

Among the faculty, some introduced themselves to me and appeared very friendly, but then the conversation turned to business, with each conversation being a variant of "My son/cousin/brother is selling a house, and if you want to buy it, they will save money on realtor's fees." This conversation occurred at least four times in my first two days, with a few more within the next couple of weeks. When I replied that I had just arrived and was not yet looking to buy, these faculty politely ended the conversation. In almost every case, they never spoke to me again.

Meanwhile, Sandra, the faculty member who had avoided any eye contact with me at the interview, studiously avoided me on campus even though we worked in close proximity. One of the other interviewers on the committee saw fit to inform me that three of the interviewers voted to hire me, and one voted to hire the adjunct. I never understood why he felt the need to tell me that.

One member of the English faculty, Esposa, who was not among my interviewers, was very sour towards me. She did not attempt any politeness, and when she did speak to me it was curt and scarcely civil. I soon learned that Esposa was the wife of the adjunct who had been promised the job, and she never hid her contempt for me. It later came to light that Sandra had been a friend of hers, but that Sandra had suffered retaliation for her participation in my interview. I do not know for certain if she voted to hire me, but for over one year after my hire her friendship with Esposa had apparently flatlined completely. As I learned, Esposa had exchanged words with her and would not speak to her afterward. This was the beginning of a decade-long vendetta against me, a vendetta which took casualties among other faculty, some of whom at times were afraid to be seen to speak to me publicly.

One year after my hire, a new president took office at McGillicuddy. In her interview, Dr. Theophage had to speak with the faculty and the staff, most of whom opposed her hire. Thom talked to me about her resume and expressed his belief that she was completely unqualified to serve as president of a college, in part because she had retired from higher education about ten years before, and had since operated a flower shop and a bed and breakfast in the Deep South. Notwithstanding the clear faculty opposition, the chancellor of the college system chose Theophage.

Theophage quicky showed herself to be a very strident white evangelical Christian. She tended to interpret matters through her religion, even going so far as talking about McGillicuddy, a state college, like a mini–Liberty University and openly talking about her church. One early convocation during her tenure featured her speaking to a captive audience of faculty and staff for fifteen minutes about how she had composed a new hymn for Jesus.

Matters at the college quickly turned sinister. Shortly after Theophage became the new president, an allegation surfaced that she had misrepresented her credentials, specifically that she had claimed a tenured position at a college for which she had never worked. William was one of the four faculty members who had sat on my interview committee, and he found himself on an *ad hoc* committee to evaluate the allegations against Theophage. He told me that he planned to support the president not because he believed her explanation (he did not) but because he and the committee hoped that this would place her in their debt. The *ad hoc* committee made their recommendation to sustain Theophage, but the committee members did not benefit the way they had hoped.

Soon thereafter, Theophage established a spy network among willing faculty and staff, and when other faculty complained, she went to war, using a "budget crisis" as an excuse to force the retirement or outright termination of many college personnel, including faculty. The "crisis" began when it came to light that someone, just retired, had misinterpreted budget projections, making the college think it had much more money than it really had. Esposa became even more powerful by cozying up to Theophage and becoming a major, and open, spy. Many faculty and staff were intimidated and went quiet around the spies, who took notes at faculty and division meetings to pass on to the president. One afternoon when I was in my dean's office, his secretary told me to speak very softly because two of Theophage's spies, including Esposa, were in the meeting room on the other side of the nearby door, and they might hear and report our conversation.

Theophage took a significant dislike to me, although I never found out exactly why. I do know that she and Esposa became close friends and attended the same Southern Baptist church along with many of the staff and some of the faculty. Oddly, Theophage could never recognize me on sight. On one occasion, she introduced me to a group of local dignitaries on campus as "Professor … um …" and then moved on to another faculty member whose name she did know. About a year and a half later, another "budget crisis" resulted in further culling of the herd. Strangely, this second budget crisis also resulted because someone had retired from the college and misinterpreted a "carry-forward" in the budget which made the college think it had much more money than it really had. If this happening one time appeared unbelievable to many in the college, then having it happen a second time appeared downright suspicious. A third, smaller, budget crisis, followed within another year or so, and once again, more faculty and staff were either retired out or laid off. Five years after Theophage had taken power, almost all faculty who had opposed her hiring, and even those who had sat on the committee that had sustained her, were gone. It became clear that any who spoke openly about her questionable credentials would find themselves in her crosshairs. One of my students asked Theophage about the tenure issue in question, only to be met with a scowl and a balled fist held tightly at her right thigh. Those faculty and staff left were either new, her supporters, or watching their backs continually.

One of the most disturbing events to me, one which caused me to second guess my future in higher education, was the termination of my officemate, Hugh. Hugh and I had already gotten to know one another well when we were moved into one large office together. He taught psychology and sociology, and we had many stimulating conversations. In fact, Hugh became the first real colleague I had at McGillicuddy, and by colleague, I mean a faculty member off of whom I could bounce ideas and consult regarding matters within his ken. Unfortunately, at McGillicuddy College, very little collegiality existed among the faculty. As one staffer told me, "At this college, they have spent years encouraging people to do their jobs, get their paychecks, and go home."

By the end of my third year, Hugh had begun to push the boundaries of his position. He organized a conference for the undergraduate students, and he began researching the culture of the college. As a minority, he took a keen interest in McGillicuddy's treatment of minorities, especially in the pay disparities between whites and non-whites. As he conducted his research, Hugh expressed to me on multiple occasions that he felt disappointment that so many of the minorities seem to just accept white attitudes about them at the college. Needless to say that many of the faculty and staff did not care for him, or as one of the administrators (all senior administrators were white) said, "We can't fire him because he's Black."

Hugh's end came, at least in part, from a bad evening. One morning he told me that he had been arrested for a DUI the night before and would need to appear at court, and that he had just come from a meeting where he had informed the administration of his situation. This occurred very close to the end of the academic year, as everybody was preparing for summer. A few days later, Hugh and I were in the office checking on our Fall schedules, when he noticed that his had been erased. He and I knew that his end was coming, which it did within another day or so. In our final conversation, he looked dejected and very depressed. Hugh could not believe what had happened, or that he had been officially terminated not for the DUI but for low student evaluations. When I returned to the office after summer, most of his possessions were still in the office, which I found odd. I later learned that his keys had been confiscated and he had been banned from the campus shortly after our last conversation. Security confiscated his possessions and held them for over a year. Just before the confiscation, two psychology instructors emailed me to request permission to enter my office so they could rifle through his books and see which they wanted for themselves. I refused this vulturine request.

That Fall semester, a whispering campaign moved through McGillicuddy College that Hugh had been fired for drinking on the job. A few faculty even told me that they had personally encountered him drunk at the college or teaching classes. This was strange, as being his officemate, I never saw him intoxicated at work, or smelled alcohol on him, and we certainly had worked together long enough. Hugh's termination and the subsequent whispering campaign killed any trust I had for the faculty, staff, and administration at the college. He later took his case to federal circuit court, and the court's preliminary findings are a matter of public record. No lawyer in the area would represent him so he approached the court *pro se*, and although he made many mistakes in representing himself, he did convince the court to proceed with a trial on two charges. Soon thereafter, McGillicuddy settled out of court. An odd comment on the matter came from an administrator: "The settlement wound up being less than he was offered when he left."

The Teaching Experience

Despite this chaos, I still had a job to do, which was to teach History and Religion. Any history professor finds students who come to class with peculiar interpretations of history. One memorable student in my U.S. History classes often interrupted to inform the class that history and government are dictated by the Bolivian Illuminati. No doubt this student meant the Bavarian Illuminati, but he stood his ground that the Illuminati arose from Bolivia. Those students who pay little to no attention in class tend to reveal themselves in their essays, such as in one essay on the Civil War which asked students to discuss Washington's program to colonize Freedmen on Île-à-Vache in Haiti in 1862—Washington as in the United States capital. Some students talked about George Washington's work in colonizing Freedmen in 1862 (although he had been dead for 63 years), and a smaller number discussed Booker T. Washington's attempts to resettle Freedmen in 1862 (at the age of seven, apparently).

Yet by far my most interesting, and memorable, encounters come from teaching religious studies. One of the most commonly encountered misunderstandings is the confusion between theology and the academic study of religion. This leads some students and faculty to assume a religious studies professor must be *ipso facto* a Christian minister, for example. At McGillicuddy College, religion classes are routinely assigned to adjuncts who are evangelical ministers, even as students complain that these preachers obviously do not know the material. More than a few students have asked why I hired adjuncts who show no interest in or knowledge of any religion other than their own, only to have them express surprise when I inform them that I have no control over the hiring of adjuncts, and no control over what they do.

I have had more than a few students inform me that their ministers have warned them against taking my religion classes. One student told me that upon informing her minister that she was taking my class, he warned her: "Remember that is *man's* understanding of the Bible, not God's." Another minister even decided to sit in on the first session of my Old Testament course, although he never intended to enroll. He spent much of the class interrupting with pearls of wisdom, such as the existence of the Coelacanth proving geologists wrong about the age of the Earth, and that the field of textual criticism should be called "Destructive Criticism." After class, he attempted to interrogate me on my religious beliefs (which I never discuss at the college), then left never to return.

Islam, unsurprisingly, has proven a most controversial topic. Two Islamic groups exist within the community, both very small. The older group is a Black Muslim congregation which is now Sunni but originated as a splinter group from the Nation of Islam. The younger group is comprised of international students recruited by McGillicuddy for its NJCAA soccer program. The international Muslims, in particular, have caused a stir. I have heard complaints that these Muslim students are allowed to pray to *their god* in school, but good Christians are forbidden from doing the same. When pressed for which Muslim students pray in college, and when, and where, nobody can answer. None who complain about this have ever actually witnessed it, and can only ever respond with "Well, I heard...."

My attempt to teach a class on Islam died quickly and quietly. Nobody enrolled. This bias against Islam even impacts the marketing of Religious Studies courses. Some professors, such as our single geologist, engaged in various forms of marketing or community engagement in order to bolster enrollment for particular classes. So I engaged in marketing Religious Studies. This was both to bolster enrollment in the classes and to clear up misconceptions, the main one being that Religious Studies classes were essentially Sunday School and were therefore easy. Incidentally, that geology instructor often found herself dealing with student complaints because she would not teach according to the Young Earth Creationism of many white evangelicals, who see the Earth as only 6,000 to 10,000 years old. She is no longer with McGillicuddy College, and her position has since been eliminated.

I and three college staff worked up a plan which involved print, social media, and television. We decided to begin with a series of "Did You Know?" factoids, which would hopefully pique peoples' interests in the topic of world religions. We knew after the third "Did You Know?" something was amiss. The college's social media page had likes and comments on every other post but these three. The fourth post caused a kerfuffle: "Did you know that Jesus is an important prophet in Islam?"

No comments appeared online, but I was informed by one staff member who worked on McGillicuddy's social media accounts that the phone lines were jammed. Angry calls from community leaders and local clergy demanded that our marketing be shut down immediately. The very idea that Jesus might be an important figure in Islam was too offensive to contemplate. The college administration immediately complied, and further orders made it clear that religious studies classes are never to be marketed to the community in any way. Word even began to leak (unverified, I might add) that certain of McGillicuddy College's major donors had complained. If this did indeed happen, and I have no evidence that it did, then it would be a sad commentary on how financial pressure can quickly and easily be used to stifle controversial fields and academic freedom more generally.

Students who are attracted to eastern and other non-Christian religions tend to avoid both Old Testament and New Testament courses. As mentioned earlier, adjuncts taught the religion classes in the years before I arrived, and all of them were either ordained evangelical Christian ministers or other church personnel. The classes gained a reputation for being little more than preaching at the college. In my Old Testament class, I cover not only all the books in the Old Testament of the Protestant churches, but works such as Greek Daniel, Ecclesiasticus, and 1–4 Maccabees. This has provoked reaction from many evangelical students who ask why we are covering books not in the Old Testament. When I reply (as I have many times) that other groups of Christians, for instance Catholics, have different versions of the Old Testament, I can always rely upon at least one student to chime in, "But Catholics aren't Christians. Why should we look at their books?"

The most conservative-minded evangelical Christian students tend to be attracted to my New Testament classes, and this is where most of the conflicts occur. It is also where most of the plagiarism and academic dishonesty occurs, almost always from the self-confessed evangelical Christian students. More liberal-minded students tend to avoid this class, and it is a pity as their voices could contribute valuable viewpoints. About five students over the past three years have sent me emails condemning me for teaching the New Testament in a way which does not accord with their churches, and one even told me that Jesus would destroy me. Quite a few students, when faced with Greek passages which do not accord with their beliefs (particularly among those who revere the KJV), declare the Greek flawed and the KJV correct. As one student informed me, "The front page of the [KJV] Bible says it's authorized. That means it's authorized by God." Anecdotes such as this one would seem to hint that among some Appalachian evangelicals, the KJV has become a fetish object.

Running Off the Rails

Six years into my employment, I was called to a meeting with the new dean, William, the same William who had helped sustain Theophage, and who had served on my interview committee. By this time, I was feeling low. The spy network was at full strength, and many faculty, especially those hired before Theophage's presidency, were cowed. On the other hand, morale was high among those who were close to the president, who herself seemed to live in clover. Esposa's husband, the adjunct who had quit mid-class when he did not get my job, had been rehired by William, who was a friend of his. About a year earlier, Theophage had informed me that McGillicuddy would no longer pay for me to travel to academic conferences as it did "not benefit the college." Other faculty continued to receive such funding, however.

William opened our meeting by saying, "You are going to be fired, but I can't tell you why." This is always an intriguing way to begin a conversation. He then informed me that the college administration had received three emails detailing accusations against me which were so serious that Theophage had ordered my immediate termination in the middle of the academic year. When I inquired after the charges in the emails, William refused to tell me, claiming that he needed to protect the privacy of the people who had made the charges. Since I was being fired anyway, I pushed back and made it clear that terminating somebody, even a faculty member under contract with the state, could present legal issues if no reason were given for the termination. He hesitated and stood his ground for about one minute, then read something on his computer screen for a few minutes. He then said that the three emails had all come from addresses not associated with the college, and then noted that all three emails were very similar in structure, with very similar charges in much the same order. He then offered the only clear accusation during that meeting: "They say you made fun of 9/11 in class." I told him that my inclination toward gallows humor notwithstanding, I never made fun of 9/11 in class. He demurred and indicated that he did not believe that particular allegation. After some more thinking on his part, he told me that all three emails pretty much agreed with one another. And the more he looked at the emails, the less confident he became. The meeting ended with William telling me that he was going back to the senior administration about the emails and the charges. That was the last I heard about the matter. I was neither fired nor reprimanded, and the matter was quickly and quietly dropped. Whenever I inquired afterward what had come of the investigation into the emails, I was always met with silence.

Months afterward, the committee on multi-year appointments met. At McGillicuddy College, faculty do not have traditional tenure but are instead given multi-year appointments, which themselves are rather meaningless since employment is based upon annual contracts granted by the president's office. I knew that I was up for a multi-year appointment and was assured that the process was pretty much automatic. William called me to a meeting in his office, where he informed me that my multi-year appointment had been rejected. When he had inquired as to why, he was told that the reasons were confidential. When he asked to appeal the committee's decision, he was told the committee had already adjourned and appeal was impossible. The next step was for me to contact HR and inquire after the issue, which I promptly did. The head of HR replied to my email request with an explanation that the committee's discussions were confidential and that in order to protect their identities, I could not be told why I was denied a multi-year appointment. Again, I pushed, only to receive a terse reply from the head of HR, "Too many negative student comments." I found that disingenuous; most of my student evaluations returned positive or neutral comments. Of course, I could always count on at least one student per year who complained that I assigned them too many essays or that my religion courses were not like Sunday School.

About two weeks later, I had a conversation with Meredith, a faculty member who had earlier befriended me and who did not fear the wrath of Esposa or Theophage. She told me that she was on the committee that denied my appointment, as was Esposa, along with other allies of Theophage. According to her account, there was no reason to refuse the appointment, but Esposa argued against me. Apparently, she convinced the committee to change the rules for the multi-year appointment specifically to deny it to me. Theophage had it within her power to review the decision and reverse it, but she refused to do so; the decision stood. I had tried to find other jobs in the meantime, but new colleges want letters of recommendation from current coworkers and administrators speaking to a faculty member's abilities and temperament, and with the exception of Meredith, nobody at the college would vouch for me lest they cross Theophage and her supporters. Meredith, unfortunately, later died from Covid early in the pandemic.

As it turned out, I was given a multi-year appointment very quietly, although I could never uncover a reason for the reversal. A few years later, I and many others at McGillicuddy were finally able to breathe on a March day nine years into Theophage's tenure. In a sudden announcement over Zoom, she declared her retirement. Her announcement included a statement of her religious beliefs and came complete with a 12-minute sermon invoking God's protection over the college. She also informed the Zoom attendees that she was planning to write a "tell-all" book about her experiences at McGillicuddy College, but so far that book has not materialized. Esposa retired with Theophage, and the rest of the college spy network dissolved.

Sandra, from my hiring committee, also retired. She returned six months after her retirement to become an adjunct. I found her friendly and chatty. She often talked of her love of New Orleans and her soft plans to move there someday. I never asked her about my interview or her avoidance of me, and she never mentioned it. It felt to me like she was free to be herself after retirement, and she could talk to whomever she wished.

Exiled Before I Began

Matthew Boedy

I was exiled from Small-Time U before I taught my first class. I was fired from the job before even signing my contract. But that is getting ahead of the more important story about my Small-Time U that helps us all better understand the larger exile in higher education.

The large majority of institutions, especially public ones, exist or are exiled to the margins of national media coverage about higher education. The Ivies and R1s are not where most of us work. My marginal school, spread across five campuses in a largely rural corner of a Southern state, offers a good picture of the promises and perils of being exiled to Small-Time U. This essay will describe those tensions amid my changing notion of what it means to work at such a place. And almost not get the chance.

I am a professor at the University of North Georgia, which was founded in 1873 in the gold mining town of Dahlonega. Following the Civil War, an abandoned U.S. Mint in what is now a wine and art tourist locale (also the setting for a hit 2017 country song) was given to the state of Georgia, which used it to start North Georgia Agricultural College. When mineral sciences as an education endeavor eventually died out, the school became a liberal arts school. It was the first college in the state to graduate females. But also through its link to the law creating land-grant universities that required military training for students, it remains one of seven senior military colleges in the nation. Throughout its more than 150 years of operation, it has been decimated by national economic trends and revived again and again by enrollment surges and funds for new construction.

I give the reader this truncated history and present picture to frame this: as a person who grew up in Georgia I had never heard of UNG before I applied for a job here. To give the reader even more of a sense of how exiled the school is, I will also note I taught high school for four years in this state, two at a school whose student body matches my predominantly white university. There are several personal reasons for my ignorance. One is as a high school graduate in suburban Augusta (about three hours away) I was a top student heading to a top university. (I graduated with a B.S. in journalism from the University of Florida in 2001.) Two, my town had a university I was very familiar with and that was very much considered lower in standard than where I matriculated. And three, while I had the opportunity (but declined) to pursue college baseball on a scholarship, my high school had never sent athletes to UNG as far as I knew. In short, I was not the kind of student this "open access institution" was looking for. UNG admits nearly 75 percent of those who apply to our bachelor or associate degree programs.

UNG is an access institution. But fewer students will be seeking access in the future. While UNG enrolls about 18,000 students, the share of high school graduates will shrink here soon. And while nearly 80 percent of our students are from a 30-county area in northeast Georgia, that area is set to take more than the average brunt from the "enrollment cliff." More than 70 percent of students are white and nearly 60 percent are female. That likely won't change. But if the trends continue, we will not remain with more than 700 full-time and about 300 part-time faculty.

Outside that real concern, I am also exiled at my own exiled Small-Time U. When lawmakers and members of the Board of Regents talk about our school, they almost always refer to the historic campus in Dahlonega. But I teach on a campus near Gainesville about 45 minutes from the mountain city. In 2012 the state merged North Georgia College with Gainesville State College, a "junior" college, to create UNG. Each school already had a "feeder" campus and eventually the school started a fifth campus near the Tennessee border. My campus doesn't have sports, a Greek system, or residence halls like Dahlonega. Also, all commencement ceremonies are on the Dahlonega campus, where the school built a new convocation center. The reader should note that students on my campus have likely never set foot on the Dahlonega campus for courses. I go up there for the food and town festivals, though hardly ever for work purposes.

While I am exiled, so is my school. Like other small schools, we are overshadowed by R1s in our state, especially the one an hour down the road from me that has recently won two national football championships in a row. (UNG does not have a football team, though our softball team won a Division II national championship in 2023.) We are also in a third "tier" of schools as designated by our university system. (In that tier, faculty teach a 4/4 course load. In comparison, faculty at two-year schools in a fourth tier often teach 5/5 for less money.) That tier means less brand awareness in the public at large. In fact, some members of our state's Board of Regents have said they like what our school produces but don't fully understand its unique mission or role in the larger university system. To be fair, these regents are chosen by where they live in the state, though that goes even more to my point that my school is exiled from the wider public consciousness within our own state.

Our school remains less known because we simply have never needed to be known more than we are. At least since the 1950s, this region of Georgia has produced a big enough crop of high school students eager for but less prepared for some form of higher education. Our lottery-funded scholarship which began in 1993 has played a big role in giving these students an opportunity. And other state funds flooded in when the merger doubled enrollment in an instant, giving UNG a better position in the system's funding formula which largely uses credit hours as its standard. That boom allowed the school to hire more faculty and offer better salaries, which persuaded me. I had other offers nationwide, perhaps less secure. I chose UNG because it was close to family and I knew the state. But in recent years recurring budget cuts and enrollment declines have made clear UNG is being impacted by larger trends affecting higher education. Schools like UNG are trying to find a path forward from exile because exile is no longer a comfortable place.

At UNG there is a sizable portion of students who mirror me as a high school student. UNG hosts many dual-enrolled students who will move on from here very soon to a bigger, perhaps better place. But I have developed a deep sympathy for those others who are not like me and remain, those whose test scores and GPA largely left them with this school as the only option. They are not less committed. Some are even more committed because many are paying their own way. But they are also part-time workers and part-time students, not known for a family history of college. More than a few freshmen are not yet 18. While I teach the overeager junior in high school, I also teach the already fully employed, the "long time ago I went to college and left" student.

These latter students are quicker than the younger ones to know the difference between bullshit a professor is peddling or the interesting offer they are making. I of course am always doing the latter. The younger students end up doing exactly what you tell them—and telling you exactly what you want to hear, per the "rubric." Both groups though are linked through my pedagogical exile. I teach the exiled subject known as rhetoric.

Rhetoric was once a college major. And our state's flagship liberal arts school (did I mention I work at another, lesser known one?) still offers it as a major. But it has long been exiled in high schools. It's taught to the Advanced Placement crowd but not to the large majority of high school students. In higher education it made a comeback in the '70s. That growth parallels of course the growth of first-year writing courses across the nation. (I wrote a short book about the impact of those trends and the link to the May 1970 shootings at Kent State and Jackson State.) First-year writing as a course has long been taught by an exiled class of instructors. Overburdened with grading papers, the majority of its instructors have been for decades either graduate students or non-tenure-track faculty, adjuncts pushed from campus to campus, exiled from the security of the job I have. I certainly recognize my status as a tenured professor. But that doesn't mean my exile at Small-Time U isn't also burdensome.

Rhetoric as an academic discipline is also often marginalized by my department colleagues who teach literature (who outnumber me 20–1). I don't begrudge them that opinion. But in the debate about the future of the English major, it's hard to get them to see the way forward. And that path must include "career-ready" writing skills, as our system likes to label them. I'm adverse to mimicking much of what the system gives us, but to fight for the future of an exiled degree program like English I'll use any rhetoric that works. And English majors are getting fewer and fewer at my school.

That leaves me closer and closer to actually being exiled from this school. Two schools in our university system that offer four-year degrees no longer have an English major. At my school English majors account for 1.5 percent of all students, half of what it was just a few years ago. We are marketing more but the major faces long-term trends not in its favor. To be blunt, I give the English major at my school ten more years before it is erased. Schools with graduate students will survive but jobs for those students will become even more scarce. Once English faculty are exiled to merely teaching general education or the required "core" classes it will be a short jump to say we don't need as many as we have now. Exile can happen fast or slow. Sometimes you see it coming and sometimes you don't.

And that brings me finally to the beginning.

The story I will detail (though not with names) will reveal the ways in which schools at the margins have to balance many pressures to attract and retain people like me. The story reflects how power gets abused by powerful people at marginalized schools who have spent years defining and defending their territory within a small, marginalized university. I happened to piss off one of those people and he fired me before I had ever taught a class.

A few days after my campus interview, I accepted an offer from my department head with a specific salary listed in an email. I thought nothing of it until weeks later when I received a call from a school administrator whom I had not met on my campus tour. (I am purposefully not using his title as that would identify him.) He told me that the school was not going to pay me what it (through the department chair's email) had promised. He refused to say why or how the decision was made. I was understandably angry and even more livid as he continued throughout our long conversation to refuse me any details. He offered to help me leave the university within a year or supply me with a "start up" fund that is not a normal part of a new position at a school like mine. (I used that fund to buy books, though I was told I could not use it to buy technology because the computer would not be mine to own.) After his refusals, he said I had to learn to trust him and other school leaders.

Once off the phone, confused and confounded, I emailed the department chair I had interviewed with, future colleagues who had hosted me, and a faculty senator, asking the same question about how this happened. All responded with confusion akin to mine. Word got back to the administrator about those emails. He called me again to angrily denounce my communications as me trying to start an "investigation" and rescinded the offer I had accepted weeks earlier. And for those not in the know like I was, since I had not signed a contract (due to the university's own incompetence with the salary issue), the administrator knew exactly what he was doing: I was jobless with no recourse.

After even more emails and now panicked calls to my graduate school advisors and future colleagues, I "humbly" emailed the administrator to apologize and asked him to reconsider. He took the weekend to do so and then sent me a terse note on Monday to say a contract would be forthcoming within the hour. I signed it.

First, let me be clear: the difference in salary between the initial offer and what I was forced to accept was marginal and I received a raise in that exact amount the next year. It was the unprofessional and disturbing behavior of the administrator after my inquiries that defined the situation for me. I never reported the incident, never spoke about it with any other administrator, and of course never with that specific administrator. In fact, I have made it my intention to avoid him at all costs. As I have learned over the years, stories about his style of leadership are legion at my school. In a hopeful note, when our school got a new president recently, this administrator was removed from management, though with a new "cushy" title and role.

After I received tenure, I filed an open records request for emails during this time period and read about what happened in real time. It remains unclear in some respects, but the salary offered to me was not in the end approved by the provost and the administrator then made that terrible phone call. Why it wasn't approved or how the salary came to be offered without approval remains a mystery. Whatever the role this administrator might have played—or missed playing—in getting a salary approved, his emails to others about me made clear he saw my concession as a victory for himself.

This story didn't end with my demise. It was the ground for my entry into faculty advocacy and solidarity work that aims to change public opinion of higher education. Since that exile-turned-entry point I have become the president of our state faculty association and an important part of a larger national group that advocates for higher education professionals. That group, the American Association of University Professors, has long been a champion for academic freedom and other campus issues. As I have learned over the years and seen in other examples, administrations and faculty sharing in principles and policies is the only way all of this works.

Even while I am protected in some ways, still I wonder what will become of this writing the reader is seeing. Will that administrator come across my words? It shouldn't be this way. I should not have been treated that way. And yet, there is fear of exile in my heart. I remain on another campus at my Small-Time U, trying to see the future of higher education amid thoughts of exile.

Making the Most of the Rest of Your Career

Confessions of a Public Historian in Southwest Georgia

Evan A. Kutzler

One evening it happened over a bowl of Brunswick stew in 2017. Former president Jimmy Carter, First Lady Rosalynn Carter, and a half-dozen other guests sat around a table in Jill Stuckey's dining room in Plains, Georgia. President Carter was in a quiet mood. Perhaps he was thinking about his Sunday school lesson the next morning. Or maybe he did not feel well. Jill tried to rekindle discussion and cheer up President Carter by mentioning the progress on a new biography.

"Evan's been doing some research for Jon's book," Jill said. "He has been reading through the school board records."

My heart stopped. In a moment, I had stopped being the curious history teacher "out at the college" as locals said. In a world of partisan politics and political legacies, a small moonlighting project might look like opposition research. I felt like a plant—a spy.

Jimmy Carter served on the Sumter County Board of Education from 1955 until 1963. Carter was not an outspoken segregationist, no Lester Maddox, but in the 1950s being a "moderate" in Georgia meant not challenging segregation either. Had Carter done so, the all-white Sumter County grand jury would not have chosen him to serve on the school board in the first place. The school board was perhaps a more dangerous subject for Carter's legacy than stagflation, the crisis of confidence speech, or Iranian hostages.

Carter looked up from his stew. At 92, he still had the steely blue eyes his aides remembered with admiration and intimidation.

"What have you found?"

"Not much," I said. "I am surprised how little explicit mention there is in the minutes of federal court rulings, integration, or white resistance."

It was a true, if incomplete, answer. The minutes showed a school board carrying on as though Brown vs. Board of Education hadn't occurred at all. This was the norm for Georgia and other southern states through the 1960s. In one meeting, Carter moved to stop construction on a new African American school because local whites complained that their children also used the sidewalk. White and Black children would cross paths on the way to school. The board approved Carter's motion, but the state pushed back because too much money had already been spent on the new school site. The school board backed down. Carter later sat quietly through the state-led hearing surveying Sumter County residents whether they would prefer closing public schools over integrating. I held my breath in the short pause before Carter's response.

"We were too busy working," Carter said.

He had already turned his attention back to the stew.

The tone and body language made it clear that his true, if incomplete, response had ended the conversation. I think I know what he meant in those five words. He was too busy working to keep public schools open when faced with the choice of keeping schools segregated (and open) or integrated on paper (and closed). It was a fragment of a grim calculus, not unlike that disembodied white moderate who Martin Luther King, Jr., criticized in his "Letter from a Birmingham Jail." I had no expectation Carter would walk me through those morally challenging years with the same energy he talked about the naval academy, his presidency, or his post-presidency. Once he said he ran for state senate to get off the school board. I believe him. Yet he faced the same challenges at least until his gubernatorial inauguration. He had to appeal to voters who elected outspoken segregationists like Roy Harris, Lester Maddox, and Richard Russell. It is understandable if Carter feared readers in the twenty-first century would not appreciate the political geography of Georgia in the 1950s and '60s.

I have often privately referred to this subject as the most important conversation I could never have with President Carter. Perhaps I was a coward for not pushing the subject. "Working on what?" I might have said. Or "Could you elaborate?" Yet I had evaded his question, too, and access—my seat at the table—came at a price. I wanted to be polite. Having proximity to someone as honest as President Carter but not being able to have a frank conversation about this phase of his life is one of the contradictions I experienced in southwest Georgia.

Scholars at small, rural state universities are likely to share my experience of other contradictions. Online databases make it easier and easier for scholars to triangulate sources, but when corporate monopolies' prices strain even the budgets of R1 and R2 institutions, it warps the axiom "publish or perish." I often had to pirate—to steal from companies like ProQuest—to publish by using other people's log-in credentials. Public dissemination is also easier than ever before but it, too, comes at a cost. The political vortex of the present tends to warp public-facing scholarship and activism, making both less effective.

Maybe it was for Carter's sake as well as mine that we could never go deeper into his school board years. Perhaps I am wrong to discuss those semi-private conversations now. Yet my personal relationship with the Carters from 2015 to 2023 predated my job at Georgia Southwestern State University and was one of the many experiences I would never have had had I landed at a larger, more prestigious university. I arrived as a seasonal park ranger with a Ph.D. at Andersonville National Historic Site in 2016 and left the region eight years later to become an associate professor at Western Michigan University.

* * *

Southwest Georgia became my "history lab" for research, teaching, and service. Part of this shift had to do with resources. During the first round of interviews in 2016, the chair of the search committee asked how much research money I would need. "Nothing," I said. After finishing my book there were opportunities for research in the university's backyard. Time also pushed me to local history. Teaching a 4/4 course load on a $44,000 salary also meant that I had little time for academic conferences or money for research trips. The job pushed me toward local history.

The local history also pulled me in. The region's challenging past paralleled that of the nation—often in exaggerated form. Along the Sumter/Macon County line was Camp Sumter or "Andersonville," a Civil War prison where 13,000 U.S. soldiers perished for want of food, clean water, and shelter over 14 months in 1864 and 1865. In Plains, Jimmy Carter became the first (future) president born in a hospital in 1924. Clarence Jordan founded an interracial Christian farm in 1942 that became the birthplace of Koinonia Partners, a partnership housing program, and, later, Habitat for Humanity International. In next-door Schley County, in 1948, an all-white jury sentenced Rosa Lee Ingram and two of her teenage children, Sammie Lee and Wallace, to death for killing a white sharecropper who attacked the African American family. Fifteen years before Civil Rights protesters marched through Albany and Americus, this region was notorious for the Ingram case. Far from exile, southwest Georgia was an incubator that let me grow my post-doctoral identity as a public historian and a scholar.

Change takes time. I spent the first three years observing and making small steps outside of my comfort zone, starting with a little research for the Carter biography. These small steps overlapped with finishing an edited collection of Civil War prison letters and a monograph on the sensory experiences of Civil War prisons. Yet even without these academic projects, the sheer scale of the region's history would have overwhelmed me. Taking with me a map of endangered properties from a 1996 survey, I drove dirt roads in September 2016 looking at the remnants of houses, churches, and schools that dated mostly from the time before the Great Migration and mechanized agriculture. I kept asking myself, a professional variation of the life lesson Jimmy Carter taught every week at Sunday School, what sort of historian do I want to be? How will I make the most of my time here?

One of my first local writings started during an active shooter lockdown on Pearl Harbor Day in 2016. I had just submitted grades when all the office phones rang at once. The recorded message stated that a shooting had taken place near the golf course, and I should shelter in place, lock doors, and stay away from windows.

Concentration eluded me. At first, I distracted myself by reading a heated Facebook debate between my uncle in Colorado and a professor at Albany State University, over the history and memory of Pearl Harbor, Tokyo, Nagasaki, and Hiroshima. It was race and memory through and through. Then I started looking for information about the shooting. That, too, became a lesson in race and memory. I learned that an African American man in his thirties had shot county sheriff Nicholas Smarr and Georgia Southwestern safety officer Jody Smith during an arrest. On Jody's fiancée's page, I found a shared video from the suspect, Minguell Lembrick, and followed the link to his page.

On Lembrick's page, the gunman's friends, family, and strangers kept descending, trying to make sense of events as they unfolded in real time. Lembrick had posted a short goodbye. "Love you all," he wrote. Then he posted a live video telling friends and family that he would miss them (he later took his own life). Confused friends and family asked questions. Some told him to delete his account, to run, to reload, not to shoot, to give himself up, or to think about his children. Many called for prayer. At least one referenced the troubled history between white officers and African Americans in Americus. Several white commenters called for quick, violent "justice." These posts included a man in uniform, apparently a soldier at Fort Benning, who threatened to kill Lembrick and any of his friends and family who supported him.

Elsewhere the sadness and anger were also palpable. A white female staff member of the student services team at Georgia Southwestern posted on Facebook that this is not the time to be "PC." The man is a "thug," she said, and not a victim. Applauding her self-restraint, a colleague wrote that she could use more "colorful" language than a "thug" to describe Minguell Lembrick. She did not have to say the six-letter word she was holding back. The implication was clear. The whole day offered a live look at gun violence in a polarized town and region. The "Back the Blue" signs that already covered the white and affluent parts of town became ubiquitous in those same places. In the process, some local whites remembered that the signs appeared only after the shooting.

The Facebook distraction turned into a writing frenzy for the rest of the lockdown. I turned to digitized newspapers and began looking into the local history of lynching to add historic context to the present outpouring of violence and vitriol. I came to the name William Redding, an African American man lynched in Americus in 1913 for allegedly shooting the police chief. Redding was hanged, shot, set on fire, and—in Booker T. Washington's summary—boiled in oil at one of the major intersections just hours after a traffic stop ignited the bloodshed. Six hours of writing later, hunger and thirst drove me to break lockdown protocol and make a break for the car with or without clearance from the school. My essay, "The Ghost of William Redding," reflected on the 2016 lockdown and the lynching 103 years earlier. I did not touch the essay for three years and never published it in its original form. When it emerged during the George Floyd protests in 2020, I rewrote it as a 6,000-word, four-part series for the local newspaper that removed most references to the 2016 murder-suicide.

* * *

Lockdown writings and backroad rambles pointed to the future direction of my research. In the late winter of 2017, I began researching the rise and fall of an African American school during Reconstruction that was somewhere on the footprint of the notorious Confederate prison of Andersonville. Serendipity intervened when the National Park Service called for proposals for a study on African American history at Andersonville up to the present. In a matter of days, and at the invitation of a colleague at the University of West Georgia who knew my Civil War era research, my internal request for $500 to travel to New Orleans became the core of a $91,000 proposal that resulted in a book-length NPS publication. This temporarily solved (many times over) the research funding problem. It seeded a dozen projects to come.

In the short-run, the Andersonville research also became part of the log jam of several book-length projects that took me until the summer of 2019 to complete. Once unsnarled, I faced a much freer choice about my future direction. Envious of scholars with long-established blogs or recurring appearances in national media platforms, I wanted to find my own outlet for smaller, bite-sized projects. Would it be a blog? A website? A serialized podcast? A series of op-eds?

Then it clicked. In June 2019, I asked the editor of the city's small newspaper whether anyone was covering the erection of a historical marker for the Savannah, Americus, and Montgomery Railway. If not, I suggested, perhaps I could submit something. By the end of the month, I had an invitation from the editor to revive the local history column. I could have up to 1,500 words or nearly a full page. For decades, county historian Alan Anderson had filled this space, but he had stopped writing years earlier. It was Alzheimer's, a cruel disease for anyone and especially so for someone so influential in preserving local memory. I started my series the month he passed.

I weighed the risks and rewards. It was unpaid. There was little to no editing by the newspaper, so I had to own all mistakes. If I wrote to please a local population, did I risk angering colleagues in my own profession? I worried about becoming "stuck" in local history. When people started calling me "the new Alan Anderson," I worried that I might become "a local historian with a Ph.D." rather than "a Ph.D. historian writing about the community." It is an important distinction. I continued the monthly series for three years. By the end, the project amounted to 65,000 words.

Blending history and journalism was one of the best decisions I made in Georgia. Over time, I came to understand that I was writing for three audiences: those residents who still bought the newspaper, anyone who found the digital copy online, and historian colleagues who might see the articles shared on social media. The challenge of writing on set deadlines changed my research and writing skills and helped develop a better writer's discipline. Over the first year, my articles included the following topics: the separation in slavery and reunification in freedom of an African American couple; the sounds of early Americus; the rehabilitation of GSW's old gym; a "haunted" house in Plains; Wreaths Across America; a Rosenwald School; the city's first KFC; a book owned by a Confederate soldier I found on the side of the road while jogging; Black prisoners of war at Andersonville; an old oral history project; and a four-part miniseries on the William Redding lynching. The articles ranged in subject, voice, and tone by design.

Thinking about a local audience led me to be more cautious in my analysis and interpretations. In September 2019, for example, I went to Leesburg, Georgia, to witness the unveiling of a Georgia Historical Society marker for the Leesburg Stockade, a concrete building where white officials locked up dozens of African American teenagers in August and September 1963. A Southern Nonviolent Coordinating Committee photographer secretly photographed the children through the bars and, over the years, the story of the "Stolen Girls" has helped connect southwest Georgia to the national Civil Rights story.

And yet historical memory divides as well as unifies. Susan Bragg, a colleague at GSW, warned me ahead of time that memories of the Leesburg Stockade divided African Americans of the Civil Rights generation. The public unveiling of the marker laid bare, for a blink of an eye, this division. Dr. Shirley Green-Reese, one of the imprisoned children and now a frequent speaker on the subject, called for any of the "the fifteen Leesburg Stockade girls" to stand up. A half dozen women stood up, including Carolyn Deloach, Juanita Freeman-Wilson, and Robertiena Freeman-Fletcher. Green-Reese recognized only one of them as being "one of the fifteen."

"And I don't see any other Leesburg Stockade girls here," she said.

Robertiena Freeman-Fletcher, a few feet away in a bright pink blazer, said she was leaving people out.

"Okay," Green-Reese said over Freeman-Fletcher. "The fifteen Leesburg Stockade girls. Any more of the fifteen Leesburg stockade girls? Okay, the fifteen girls are all honored today. Also please find a list of the fifteen Leesburg stockade girls printed on the back of your program."

I walked over to Lee Kinnamon and signaled to meet me in the stockade. Lee, now the mayor of Americus, had brought his A.P. U.S. History class to watch the unveiling. No stranger to local history, Lee looked startled. From the shade and semi-privacy of the cement prison, we took a break from the ceremony to discuss what was happening. Those in charge of the ceremonies only wanted to honor the people in the photographs. The photographs captured one day of seven weeks; as a moment in time, it happened to leave out many children whose families had apparently been able to get them released earlier. Juanita Freeman-Wilson and Robertiena Freeman-Fletcher were the daughters of a leader in the local civil rights movement. Carolyn Deloach was the daughter of Staley High School's principal. Deloach may have been cast out of the memory for an additional reason. As an adult, she left Georgia and spent her career in Chicago before returning to Atlanta to volunteer with the Americus-Sumter County Movement Remembered Committee. A combination of factors—photographic evidence, class privilege, town "loyalty"—affected the memory of the Leesburg Stockade.

When we emerged from the stockade, Green-Reese had circled back to the earlier standoff. She wanted to dispel myths about the stockade. "You cannot produce a true story unless you have facts," she said. "So if you have some pictures or some documentation that you were in that stockade, you need to do your own story. No one is saying you were here or there, but you have to write your own story." After the ceremony, the two women from the 1963 photographs, and a family member of a third, took photographs with Todd Groce of the Georgia Historical Society. The five women who Green-Reese cut out from the ceremony took their own photographs in front of the marker. Back in Americus, later that day, I spoke with Deloach to better understand what had happened outside of my hearing.

The event shaped the selection and telling of local histories for the local newspaper. It also underscored that local history was no less complex than state, national, or transnational histories. One must connect to broad themes without losing local nuance or creating stereotypes. Over time I developed a richer sense of historical complexity and an appreciation of humility when looking back from the present. While I trusted Deloach and Freeman-Wilson and believed their public humiliation has been unjust, I was never satisfied that I had pulled back all the complicated layers of the Leesburg Stockade to write about it for a local audience. Even well-intentioned writings can cause harm within the very communities I wanted to support—and whose support I needed. As with the conversation I could never have with Carter, the standoff at the marker became a go-to reminder about proceeding with caution.

* * *

Leaving southwest Georgia in summer 2023 was easy—and heartbreaking. University politics would have been enough. As chair of the university committee on academic affairs from 2019 to 2021 and president of the Faculty Senate from 2022 to 2023, I became convinced I would outlive the history program. The administration had already deactivated the B.A. in Theatre, the B.S. in Geology, and all the students who wanted to become high school teachers had been administratively moved from the College of Arts and Sciences to the College of Education. In 2016, a student could pursue a B.A. in History (and several other majors within Arts & Sciences) with a teaching certificate from the College of Education. Starting in 2022, a student could only pursue a B.S. in Secondary Education (College of Education) with an emphasis in history or other Arts and Sciences major. The decision came down to an internal presidential decree that made no wave at all. The term planned obsolescence came to mind. I had applied for other jobs as early as the fall of 2020 when most of the faculty returned to face-to-face teaching during Covid. Fearing future program cuts, I doubled down in 2022.

The job was not the only reason I left southwest Georgia. I feared my daughter's education would suffer because my career had put us in a place where the *New York Times* still covers the public-vs.-private-vs.-public charter school battles. She had wonderful friends at the Methodist church daycare, but what would happen when almost her entire preschool class went to 4-K at Southland Academy never to attend public school? I had written about the origins of the school for the local paper. It was founded in 1965 to keep prayer in the classroom and give white parents a segregated option. This left two choices. She could go to the public charter school, but I did not believe in the school's zero-textbook curriculum. Or she could go to the underfunded public school—segregated now almost as completely as sixty years ago—and be one of the only white students. What was the ethical choice? How would my wife and I explain this to my daughter? Could we respect her wishes if she disagreed with us?

I am lucky to have worked at Georgia Southwestern. No one is guaranteed even one tenure-track job in the humanities and without that first tenure-track job there could not have been a second or third tenure-track offer. My family and I talked as much about future non-academic careers as we did about the possibility of an academic move. In 2022, I took an online real estate course with the hope that I might be able to spin storytelling, historic preservation, and development into a new career. Making the most of southwest Georgia meant writing with an urgency that these might be my most creative years and the rest of my academic career might be a short one. In the process, I came to love the region, its people, and the difficult history that seemed to separate and connect everyone and everything.

Please do not confuse the above reflection with advice on how to write one's way out or pull oneself up by their own bootstraps. Most of these projects began before I became a father. I had no student loan debt, no car loan, a two-income household, and a tiny monthly mortgage payment. I could say hell no to teaching summer classes even after the NPS money ran out. I am also, by all outward appearances, a cis-gender white male. Even people who felt deeply offended by my writing accepted me as an equal citizen and accepted my right to free speech. No one to my knowledge tried to fire me. And who knows what will happen at Western Michigan University?

Casting my bucket into local history, though, offered me opportunities that greatly enhanced my love of the place that fate or chance brought me. I came to know an important and diverse swath of a community unlike anywhere I had ever lived before. The people who stopped me on the streets to say they enjoyed my work outnumbered the rare insult on the phone, in the paper, or to a mutual friend. Many who disliked one of my local public history projects appreciated others. That is as it should be. And while I feared that my daughter might one day pay a social price for my work, our social calendar was always full. My research (re)focus at Georgia Southwestern allowed me to permeate that frequent divide between the college or university and the town or region. The rewards far outweighed the costs.

Life on I-57

Place, Placelessness, and the Commuting Academic

CAMDEN BURD

Construction on I-57 began in earnest in the late 1950s after passage of the Federal-Aid Highway Act. The bill called for the creation of a new highway system that would connect the country in a vast web of concrete corridors. Arguments from engineers, government officials, and boosters abounded as to the advantages of this new system. The roads would ease urban congestion by expanding opportunities for residential development on the outskirts of cities. Military preparedness would be improved—an ever-present concern in the early days of the Cold War. Economies would expand too. No longer burdened by countless small towns and stop signs, people and goods would be able to move freely across the landscape. I-57 was completed in 1971, creating a seamless path that stretched over 350 miles from Chicago, at the northern end of the state, into Missouri after crossing the Mississippi River at Illinois' southern edge. Today, the road is a major throughway in the region, transporting people and commodities across the American Midwest.

These are historical and geographic facts—cold and clinical. Described this way, highways like I-57 are simply representations of high modernism, engineered to ease congestion and maximize efficiencies. They lack humanity. They lack meaning. But throughout history roads and paths were so much more than simply a route between two points. That was the position of geographer J.B. Jackson. During the postwar period of massive infrastructural expansion, Jackson sought to demonstrate that the path *was* the experience. The geographer worried that the arguments of engineers and planners, those prophets of efficiency, too easily paved over the ways in which humans actually related to those roads. Paths were sometimes spaces for religious encounters, sites of danger, or deep personal reflection. In an aptly titled essay "Roads Belong in the

Landscape," Jackson argued that historically, "the road offered a journey into the unknown that could end up allowing us to discover who we were and where we belonged" (*A Sense of Time, a Sense of Place*, Yale UP, 1994). But while the geographer observed that contemporary planners sought to erase the experiential aspect of the roadway, he ignored the simple truth that even the brutal and hyper-efficient superhighway still offered a *"private* experience."

That was certainly true for me. From 2019 to 2024, while an Assistant Professor of History at Eastern Illinois University, I spent a great deal of time commuting from my home in Chicago, where my partner worked, to campus in Charleston roughly 180 miles to the south. I-57 was, of course, the defining path of my commute, the road that brought me from point A to point B. Yet the highway also served as an important symbol of my academic experience. It became a consuming symbol of my struggle to find any semblance of balance between my personal life and professional pursuits. I-57 was hardly *just* a road. It had become its own place—a site for reflection on my relationship to academia.

Long commutes have their own way of working on the mind. They are more commonplace than the "road trip"—that canonical cornerstone of American popular culture. It is not a trip into the unknown. Rather, commutes are routine, almost ritual. In knowing the destination and the route, a commuter begins to see a landscape in new light. Driving to Charleston, I would merge onto the highway leaving Chicago. It was a smooth ride—a perk of the perpetual reverse commute. Chicago at rush hour can be hell, but I never knew it that way. As I left the city, I watched the urban landscape turn into a suburban one, then exurban, then rural. One can spend an entire career studying the nuances of Midwest geography, but a drive out of Chicago is its own academic experience.

Moving from Chicagoland into the vast region known as Illinois, I encountered several landmarks notable only to me. These were curios and a set of associations that I had imbued with personal meaning—a little map of my mind. For example, South of Kankakee there is a Love's Travel Stop. They have clean bathrooms and reliably carry that flavor of Doritos I like (Spicy Sweet Chili). It's not the cheapest place for fuel, though. That would be in Tuscola. Careful though. One might be tempted to stop at the gas station on the west side of I-57—the one with larger signage and sleeker aesthetics. No, one must go a bit further, past the underpass to the smaller station on the east side. Big oil can't fool me. At another point I pass an exit for Buckley, Illinois. "Buckley—like William F. Buckley," I thought to myself. "Fuck *that* guy."

The geography that surrounds much of I-57 is not an especially beautiful stretch of Earth. It was David Foster Wallace, a native of central

Illinois, who in a 1996 WBUR interview described the landscape as so flat that it "looks ironed." This reality is the product of nineteenth-century settler colonists and twentieth-century agriculture conglomerates who went to work on the land. They chopped, burned, drained, and plowed. They took a tall-grass prairie ecosystem, once abundant with various flowers, fauna, and vast wetlands, and transformed it into a flat, monotonous, drained, and commodity-rich agricultural landscape. Today, many downstate Illinoisians joke that the region is defined by two main ecosystems: corn and soy. The stretch between Champaign and Charleston is especially treeless. One has not known the horizon until they have driven through this stretch of country. Sometimes, I was convinced that if I squinted hard enough, I could see the top of the Vigo County Courthouse in Terre Haute, Indiana, nearly 80 miles away. After three hours of driving, my back was tight, my sciatica was screaming, and I was mentally drained. This was not ideal because at that exact moment office hours began.

The commuting academic is a common feature of modern higher education. I knew many faculty—mostly new hires—who commuted far distances in an attempt to balance their personal life with their professional obligations. One friend has a similar three-hour commute, traveling from his home in Minneapolis to a regional comprehensive university in Wisconsin. Another spent a year driving between New York City to a SLAC in Maine—a mind-boggling six hours on the road. Both of these were quite insignificant commutes compared to another colleague who regularly flew from New York City to Los Angeles for his position. Because of the abysmal job market for Ph.D.s, those few who are offered positions are often obliged to take them regardless of geography. They do this for many reasons. For some, it's an economic necessity. For others, it's the professional realization of nearly a decade of academic training. It's not as if there are an abundance of other options available either. For all the contemporary discourse on "Alt-Ac," few doctoral programs are adequately equipped to prepare graduates for non-academic work. Regardless of their reasons, new faculty from all over experience commute in ways that reorient themselves to home and work. I-57 was a road with particular value to me. But each commuting academic has their own places of significance. They might be rural backroads, airport terminals, and rail stations. Those roads and routes act as meaningful symbols of their academic identities.

The commuting lifestyle felt like a continuation of a particular "grind" mindset that I had adopted early in graduate school. Intimately aware of the abysmal job market for history Ph.D.s, I spent my entire graduate career taking on increased workloads, pursuing all writing opportunities, and applying to any relevant fellowships that I thought might improve my employability. I hoped to build a CV that required the prestige junkies to look past the schools that I hadn't attended and force hiring committees to spend a few moments longer with my materials before moving on to the next application. There is no question that I normalized harmful work habits. I worked long hours, withheld sleep, and ate poorly. Worst of all, though, I had convinced myself that a significant degree of suffering was required for an academic career.

Of course, this thinking was wrong. There is no such thing as "bootstrapping" your way into a tenure-track job. And though the contours of academia weren't always visible to the graduate-student version of myself who was singularly focused on "the job," I came to learn them quickly. The job market is more like a lottery; everyone tries to collect as many tickets as possible. Because most academics still value prestige above all, those applicants from a handful of programs begin with more than the rest of us. You might pick up a few more along the way but in reality, the whole thing is a matter of chance. Timing, budgets, and the innumerable biases of hiring committee members have far more of an impact on academic hiring than the countless variables that anxious applicants imagine for themselves. That fact was certainly true in my case. Given the gap between the time that had passed between my interview and the offer, I fully understood that I was not the department's first choice. The only reason I got my job at Eastern Illinois University was because at least one other person did not want it. These aspects of the job market have always existed, to be sure. But in an age dominated by institutionalized austerity and business-brained administrators, such factors are especially pronounced.

Though roads can be a place in and of themselves, their overbearing presence for commuters can have a disorienting effect. This is a sort of a dilemma. If the road becomes a central organizing geography of the mind, what does that mean for the other *places*? In my experience, I-57 had reoriented my relationship to both destinations on either end of the commute—my home in Chicago and my place of employment in Charleston. Because my assigned teaching duties would vary from semester to semester, I would spend anywhere from three to five days in Charleston. This meant that during some semesters, I would only spend three nights a week at my home. Does that even qualify as a home? Time away from my partner also made me irritable, depressed, and anxious. My physical health suffered too. I exercised less due to the commute and my consumption of junk food increased (recall the Doritos). I soon experienced intense bouts of insomnia that struck worst on the nights before I would drive south. Similar to the "Sunday scaries," the "central Illinois scaries" occurred with more frequency as the initial enthusiasm of "landing the job" gave away to the more accurate realization that this job was, in fact, a job.

The situation was not much better at the other end of I-57. Though I worked hard to ingratiate myself into the department, I always worried that my transience would be a mark against me. Unable to schedule meetings on those days when I was in Chicago, I was convinced that my colleagues considered me a flight risk, a new hire constantly on the lookout for a new job (they have not been entirely wrong). I also grew increasingly concerned that my discontent might manifest itself in the classroom. It would have been easy enough to direct that dissatisfaction towards students, an unfortunate route taken by many educators who feel the structural realties of modern academia thumping on their backs. But many students enrolled at institutions similar to Eastern Illinois University already bore the bruises of the twenty-first century. Nearly 40 percent of enrolled students were food insecure and bouts of homelessness were not uncommon. An even larger share of students juggled responsibilities increasingly common to those enrolled at regional comprehensives: tending to sick parents, caring for children, and working multiple jobs. Building a curriculum that is suited for that classroom requires compassion, not a cop. A part of me felt that I couldn't give what was necessary to teach in this environment—at least not while commuting. In an effort to embed myself in this community, I tried several living situations in the hopes that I might find a balance between my life in Chicago while establishing myself within the region. This was not an easy task. One year, I rented a university apartment which also served as a Covid quarantine for sick students. Another year, I rented a room from a colleague who lived in a nearby town. This was hardly an ideal situation as it created a sort of double commute from my home, to work, to rented apartment, to work—more time on that dreaded road.

During my final year at Eastern Illinois University, I rented a dorm room on campus. Due to declining enrollments, university administration had dedicated an entire floor to traveling faculty and potential conference attendees in an effort to offset lost revenue. The dorm room was the most affordable option—complete with two desks and twin XL beds outfitted with sheets provided by a colleague's teenage son who had attended band camp in the same building the previous summer. I was a 35-year-old academic with hand-me-downs from a thirteen-year-old. Because I wasn't eager to be *that* faculty member who was seen hanging around the dorm when most students were present, I squirreled myself away in my office for long hours until campus fell silent. Only then would I go to my room. In the meantime, I would continue those unhealthy work habits that I had established during graduate school: read more; write more; apply more; work more. The reorientation to work that I should have embraced by landing one of the few tenure-track jobs in the country never occurred. Instead, I just kept grinding. I am not entirely sure what I had imagined out of a career in academia when I started graduate school in 2012, but I know it wasn't whatever I was doing at Eastern Illinois University. Something had to give.

A faculty strike in Spring 2023 did not help things. In the months leading up to the collective action, it became clear that university administrators were pursuing the well-worn path of all bosses: seek to compel employees to work more hours for less pay. Hoping that faculty at Eastern Illinois University were already beaten down by the realities of higher education, the administrators imagined that faculty would eventually cave. We didn't. The strike was both the high point and low point of my time at Eastern Illinois University. As a committed leftie, I was happy to march alongside colleagues as a means of democratizing the workplace. A union, as far as I can tell, is the only form of "shared governance" that works on a modern college campus. It is also the best place to meet colleagues. A young faculty member can spend three years trying to find community by attending orientation, faculty meetings, and fulfilling ever-increasing committee-service requirements. But you will never meet as many like-minded co-workers until you go on strike. A picket line is a joyous, anxious, upsetting, and loving place. It's where you meet comrades; it's also where you learn how little your boss thinks of you. In my case, it also served as a break from the commute. Six days on the picket line saved me, if only for a few days, from that abysmal stretch of road.

After a few years at Eastern Illinois University, I adopted the idea of eventually leaving. My initial plan—concocted while driving on I-57—was to step away from my position after receiving tenure. The milestone would be mostly a symbolic gesture, a final CV line and capstone to my academic career. At that point, I would find other work. Perhaps some administration-adjacent position somewhere in Chicago? K-12 education? Insurance sales? Whatever. It's not exactly as if I would be leaving behind large sums of money by stepping away from a position at a regional comprehensive university. Despite working with pleasant colleagues, I had come to realize that the position was not worth the mental, emotional, physical, and familial stress. The plan represented a dwindling enthusiasm for academia that was undoubtedly shaped by my long-distance lifestyle.

But that moment of departure never arrived. In winter of 2023 I won the lottery, again, and started a new position at Clemson University a few months later. Upstate South Carolina offered a variety of opportunities that my partner and I would never find in rural Illinois: professional prospects, hills, water, and, most importantly, the chance to live together. I still have a commute, but nothing compared to that I-57 drive.

Though no mid-twentieth century planner ever imagined my particular commute in their initial plans for I-57, I find myself thinking of them and their road often. Not because I appreciated their efforts. Whereas they saw a seamless road as the pinnacle of efficiency, I saw it as drudgery. I never embraced their faith in high modernism, a quasi-religious outlook that could transform a concrete path into a symbol of progress. I found no providence in their pavement. No, I-57 stuck with me because it was a site of intense personal reckoning. It is exactly what Jackson meant when he described the "private experience" that countless individuals attached to paths and roadways—even those brutalist superhighways crisscrossing the American landscape. I-57 was more than a simple north-south road stretching the length of Illinois. It was a place where I grappled with the nature of academia and its impact on my personal relationships. It was a space that, for the first time since graduate school, forced me to contend with the blunt realities of a career in higher education.

"Roads no longer merely lead to places," Jackson wrote decisively, "they *are* places." Perhaps this is a fact lost on many, but not the commuting academic. They are all too aware that the road—their I-57—is a defining aspect of their place and placelessness in higher education.

"Wherever You Go, There You Are"
Finding Myself in Academia
Elizabeth Tacke

As I took the exit, I hoped the rundown buildings and single-story motels and fast-food joints grouped together in large stretches of flattened cornfields might signal the "outskirts" of town, and I'd find myself, soon enough, in a more recognizable Quaint College Town.™ I had elected to drive the six hours for my campus visit and had long left any semblance of civilization as I knew it. As I drove, I searched expectantly: Where was the cute bookshop? The café? Was there a brewpub maybe? Where did the faculty hang out?

A year later, I had the opportunity to teach Neil Gaiman's *American Gods*, and realized that at least the rural terrain of Charleston, Illinois, gave our class insights into the regional, rural landscape of the novel. Although I'd read the novel before, Gaiman's descriptions of small towns were now intimately recognizable: the nondenominational cemetery on the edge of town with competing funeral homes, the dying Main Street, the frequency of small-town signage on endless interstates introducing passersby to "another Town, pop. 300, home of the runner-up to the State Under-12s speed-skating championship" (152).

When the only indie bookstore closed its doors during the pandemic, I was once again reminded of Gaiman's novel: "What I say, is a town isn't a town without a bookstore," the character Hinzelmann tells us. "It may call itself a town, but unless it's got a bookstore, it knows it's not foolin' a soul" (224).

In our class discussions, I confessed to students that I had a lot to learn about myself and rural America—many students saw Charleston, IL as a bustling metropolis compared to their one-traffic-light towns. Gaiman's tongue-in-cheek descriptions of the rural midwest made me feel seen in my own experience of them, and so when I talked about teaching the novel later with friends and family, perhaps, they too might see me and help me to make sense of the new life I'd found myself in. You see, I'd "made it." I'd finished my Ph.D. and gotten the nigh-impossible tenure-track job. I didn't know how to articulate my feelings of loneliness and disillusionment.

* * *

I pestered a number of colleagues and academic friends about how to approach this essay. Perhaps I was seeking permission or solidarity in what I felt I wanted and needed to say about negotiating these past four years as an Assistant Professor at a regional university in an impoverished red stretch of central Illinois. One friend said the opening had a twinge of "coastal elitism" to it, and she's not wrong. I used to joke that I'd used the term "flyover country" one too many times in my twenties and now karma had come for me.

I moved to Charleston, Illinois, population roughly 19,000 people, in the early months of a pandemic where I bought a small house for $59,000, the down payment mostly saved from my tutoring side hustle as a Ph.D. student. My friends jokingly called it my five-dollar house. This was one of the only good things about living in Charleston, aside from the university itself. In a desperate search for community, I participated in monthly lunar sound baths that were free to the community at the Tarble Arts Center. I took a ceramics course with undergrads to scratch an artistic itch. I even tried to immerse myself in townie experiences: I played bingo every Thursday night at the local Moose lodge and sang karaoke in the downstairs cinderblock bar that shared a parking lot with the local police station.

In 2020, when I arrived, many small businesses were closing their doors, and four years later, many of those same buildings have remained empty husks. On the street I lived for two years, a neighbor's house tilted precariously to the right and in summer kids would run up and down the street barefoot with dogs off leash—a scene that always made me think of the Cunningham child in *To Kill a Mockingbird* who pours syrup all over his dinner, to Scout's horror. It was simultaneously an oddity, a story to text to friends and a reminder of the culture shock I was enduring. I used to sit on my front porch and watch all manner of atypical vehicles pass by the house: various farming devices on wheels, a unicycle, homemade electric bikes, even a motorized tricycle pulling a wagon one evening, a large American flag billowing behind it. Later, someone from town told me it was because everyone had DUIs, a remark that left me skeptical and sad at the same time.

On and off election seasons, Trump and Blue Lives Matter signs sprout up like weeds. There's enough of a tension between the "town and gown" folks to be recognizable, but the university is the main employer in the area alongside a local health center, and I've been told relations have improved over time. A student in one of my early composition courses wrote about growing up in the small town and hearing folks remarking on how the town "got dirtier" when classes would start up—a less than subtle racism remarking on the influx of students of color from other areas of the state that is engrained structurally here, just like it is across America. There's something about the small-town politics, however, that change the feel of it, at least from the perspective of a privileged White academic. The town police cars are emblazoned with "In God We Trust!" and the local sheriff has a Facebook account that posts mugshots of those residents and visitors who come into contact with "the law." I've seen way too many of our students pulled over by more than one cop car for—what appears to be—"walking while Black."

In those first two years, I reflected a lot on my own biases and assumptions about small towns and rural America. I also experienced a sense of guilt for the complex feelings I had about where I was living. I wanted to be positive and make it work. But, two years in, I opted to join most of my department colleagues and move up to the comparatively bustling area of Champaign-Urbana—colloquially known as Chambana—home of the University of Illinois and about an hour's commute north of campus.

* * *

I put off writing this essay for months, as I pondered how to approach it. In spring of 2024, my 17-year-old cat passed away after several months of being ill. I'd gotten him as a kitten the summer before my senior year of college in New York City, and his passing—coupled with a nasty bout of Covid and an exceptional chronic fatigue flare—put me into existential crisis mode. It wasn't my age that made me have a moment—at 37, I'm not old. It was the fact that this cat had seen me from a high of college-level big dreams and living in big cities to where I was now: in the middle of a corn field in central Illinois with very little community and a dragging sense of purpose.

The long and the short of it is, I'm really fucking lonely. I don't have roots in any one place because I've been constantly on the move my whole life. And I signed that contract willingly because there was always a next destination on the path I'd forged. So, I got used to starting over and figuring it out. I despised the flat, cold grey of Michigan when I first moved there from Oakland, California, for my doctoral program. (Looking back, I didn't yet know what flat truly is). But I was integrated into a community of grad students, all in the same proverbial boat. And yes, Ann Arbor was smaller than what I was used to, but it was there I realized if I had just enough variety of things to do and a good group to do it with, I was more flexible than I'd previously thought.

Since 2020, I find myself being a broken record often, initiating conversations about work/life balance, purpose, self-care, careers, community. I have these conversations with friends and family, old and new, academic and not. I know I do it too much. I've become obsessed. My whole life track has been a series of next steps and now I've found myself at the end of my map. I've started to police myself and question my incessant return to these topics.

What is my identity if I'm removed from friend groups and locations that have informed my sense of self?

* * *

I'm torn between two major realities, I realize. I love aspects of being an academic; teaching is a fundamental piece of my identity. I like my particular job too, for the most part. I've heard far too many higher ed horror stories, and while those *do* exist on my campus as well, I have a very supportive chair and a good department. I've made some friends. I get to teach a variety of courses. Our students are inquisitive and down-to-earth and hardworking. I'm on the tenure track. I have a 3–3 in a world of increasingly higher and higher course loads. I make enough to live comfortably as a single, childless person (in central Illinois), and have summer teaching opportunities for some extra financial wiggle room. I teach in a blue state and have no problems including critical race theory and discussions of prison abolition in my classes. I have the privilege of teaching in prison as part of our degree-granting program most semesters—a part of my work I have long been committed to. Do I want to be paid more? Yes. Do I want to be on 11–12 committees every year? No. Do I wish I had reliable research and travel funding and more time to commit to my writing? Yes. But there are gives and takes in this career, and for a gig at a regional rural university, I have it pretty good.

But how much of my life should be my job?

* * *

The past many years I've had an interest in learning to read tarot, which now means I have a collection of texts, a subscription to an online class I've yet to click on, and a growing number of decks I like. In my ongoing quest for making sense of who I am, tarot seemed productive. I love storytelling and a good analytic lens. But here there was also a sense of the mystical—some access to a power that I could cede control to. Perhaps the cards could give me an insight I couldn't quite grasp otherwise.

On my commutes I started to listen to tarot podcasts, but so often they are set up to be interactive, and thus I couldn't pull out the eight of wands and study it in response to the host's imperative as I drive up and down I-57. I'd pull cards sometimes before bed—self-care books told me I needed ritual—but my analytic brain wanted to memorize meaning instead of yield to inspiration. There was a correct approach, and I didn't have the time in the day to commit to study. I began to rebrand tarot in my head as an academic exercise.

When I talk to friends who I feel live their lives in technicolor, I think about what I'm doing wrong. I think about my shelves of tarot books, untouched, and the new season of *The Bear* I'd just binged. I'm not sure if my problem is that so much of my work requires reading and writing, two things I used to call hobbies. I don't know what to call them now, because when someone asks me what I do for fun, and I reference reading or writing, it usually feels like work talk. And often, it is.

I loved the semester-long ceramics course I took at Eastern my second year, but the commitment amounted to far more time than a typical hobby—easily more than 25 hours in the studio a week with classes and making time. Teaching three preps—including a teaching methods and composition course—meant that the only two things I did that semester were grade and then go to the studio and clutch a spinning wheel with my knees until 2 a.m.

I've also come to realize that I'm either 100 percent in or 100 percent out. I can't audit a "for fun" art class and not seek to master the wheel in one term. I've completely bought into the idea of academic work as a calling, and I've had pummeled into me over the years the now well-internalized belief that capacity = worth. In turn, I'm very aware of this internalized belief and then feel worse about connecting my labor to worth, and my inability to stop doing so. When the concept of "quiet quitting" took hold a couple years back and people began to, again, shake their fists at millennials, I often joked about what that would even look like for this job with its ever expanding and precarious boundaries.

As my "for work" pile of books grows, the more guilt I feel when I pick up a "for fun" book, even if that "for fun" book will surely impact my teaching, my thinking, my writing, and my sense of self. Part of the problem is I don't know how to establish boundaries between work and "not work" when everything I do *is* work. I am expected to write and publish, but one could easily argue I'm not paid to do it. My contract hours are already overwhelmed by teaching, I still fit in countless committees, and my writing is backburnered to spots on holidays and weekends or late-night binge revisions. Maybe I'm secretly afraid that if I do learn to read tarot well, I'll simply have to teach a college course on the Rhetorics of Tarot and another thing I yearn to do that is not "work" will now fit under the "work" category and more of my identity will be consumed by the academic label.

* * *

Now, up in Champaign-Urbana, I have some cute coffee shops, a brewpub. I'm in that Quaint College Town™ I'd desired earlier. But I'm still battling an undercurrent of ennui that I'm unsure what to do with. And now I have an hour commute down to my office.

Two years ago, I applied for a regional college position closer to where I grew up, and just under three hours north of where my sister and her family live. I got the campus visit. And I know if I had fit myself into the cookie cutter of the job description just a bit more, I likely would have gotten the job. But I wanted the flexibility and access I have in my *current* job at this new campus—a location on the west coast that felt like home. I took the advice of a mentor who said I needed to be myself on the market, because I didn't want to land a new job that would force me to have to cut off some of the pieces of what make me happy in academia. And, despite the cost of living being roughly 100 percent higher in the new location, the pay would have been the same. I chose to play up the parts of me that operated outside of the confines of the job ad (even if I had the expertise for the job requirements). I think about that choice often, as I watch my niece and nephew grow up over FaceTime. When people ask me about me, I spend a lot of time talking about my job. I don't know if that would be different if I privileged other aspects of my life. But can I privilege those aspects in this career? In this location?

* * *

Yet, I am beginning to find community in unexpected places.

At my retired neighbor's birthday party, I find myself pounding the table synchronously with seven queer women in their 80s to place our bets for a competitive game of "Seven Up, Seven Down." A moment of panic comes across the face of the woman across from me, a retired professor. Her watch is attempting to call 911 because our pounding triggered the fall risk detection built into her device. We wipe away tears of laughter as the watch is passed to and fro, fingers seeking to swipe away the AI notice to seek assistance.

In a prison classroom we are celebrating the end of term with a game of pterodactyl—an early improv game that immediately quashes all sense of decorum. In a circle of matching faded state blues, grown men take on child-like impersonations of dinosaurs and get into cawing matches. You can't show your teeth, or you're out. But it's hard to keep your teeth hidden when you're struck by belly-deep laughter. On more than one occasion

I've been "cawed" at by an unknown man, as I walk the silent sidewalks between prison buildings.

A colleague invites me to a summer parks and recreation cardio-drumming course. Half of the class ends up being immediate department colleagues. You can't talk shop when you're trying to follow complex choreography and hit an exercise ball with a pair of drumsticks to the beat of Tina Turner.

My politics are all over my office door at school, and I receive an invite from a group of students I've never met to talk about prison abolition over greasy slices of Dominos.

We walk in the hot sun in long oval circles, pointing at particularly witty strike signs. It's early April and we've been on strike for a few days after working without a contract since the beginning of the academic year. Whenever we pass the president's office, we clang our UPI-green cowbells. Apparently, he's been particularly annoyed with that sound. Our students are on the strike line with us. Many of them come from blue collar families, work long hours themselves outside of classes. I meet more folks that week than I have in the three years I've been at Eastern.

* * *

Recently a mentor was discussing my current book project with me as I reflected on possible presses. As I rattled off a few names from my list, they interrupted, asking if a particular press would satisfy tenure needs at my institution. "I know it's icky," they started, "but …" I assured them any academic press would be fine. Our regional university makes moves to pride itself on research—and there are folks doing wonderful, important work here—but without the funding to back it up, we can't gatekeep the way a typical R1 might. And that's healthy too.

This mentor, and others, are the same ones who remind me that my book is my "ticket out," and I think about that often. What does that ticket give me? In less than two short years, I'll (hopefully) have achieved the privilege of wearing the "golden handcuffs of tenure." The other night over drinks with a colleague in another department who has applied to any possible job they can, I discussed the possibility of going on the market in the fall to seek out those proverbial greener pastures. It might be my last chance to find myself that "perfect" job. But I'm also convinced it doesn't exist. We're always going to be making sacrifices. The other side is never going to be as green as we think it will be.

* * *

I pull a short two-card spread from a zine I picked up the last time I was on the west coast visiting my sister. The spread asks:

1. What from my past self is influencing my present self?
2. What from my future is influencing my present self? (Penrose)

I've pulled two Major Arcana cards: The Moon and The Lovers.

I laugh because the Moon, I know, is all about intuition. I try to tune into my own: the moon looks down on a winding path that begins in distant mountains, bookended by two ominous towers. The path continues, cutting between two wolf-like dogs before ending at the edge of a pond. At the bottom of the card, half in, half out of the water, sits a crayfish. There's something to intuit here about liminality and choices and journeys.

My mind wanders.

Outside the window of The Literary—my favorite local bookshop meets coffee shop meets community space—I see someone in a fluorescent orange "Free Angela" shirt wearing black Docs; their friend has The Fool tattooed on their forearm. There is so much potential for community all around me.

I've always thought about my past as a map, a checklist of next steps. We go where we get into graduate school. We go where the job is. What might it mean to reorient that journey through a lens of intuition? Might it give me more of a sense of control over where I've landed?

I turn to the second card. The Lovers is about balance, alignment. The angel Raphael looks down on Adam and Eve in the garden. He seems to be blessing them, perhaps inviting harmony between opposing forces. Or is it about making a choice, again? I always tell my students that we live in a both/and world, my way of asking them to turn away from binary thinking and sit with dissonance more productively.

My first year at a summer camp when I was quite young, we woke up at the crack of dawn, painted mud on our faces, and filled empty soda bottles with rocks to hunt a snipe. Later, when I realized I was duped, I wasn't angry. The chase had been fun. Now that the chase is over, perhaps I need to find some time to mourn, sit with nostalgia, reckon with my romanticized idea of what arrival was supposed to feel like. In his book *Wherever You Go, There You Are*, Jon Kabat-Zinn offers an introduction and rationale for mindfulness practices. He writes: "We all too easily conduct our lives as if forgetting momentarily that we are *here*, where we already are, and that we are *in* what we are already in. In every moment, we find ourselves at the crossroad of here and now" (9). What does it mean to reckon with who I am and what I want *in* the here and now?

A simplistic read of The Lovers might suggest that my future self has found balance, but the cards are not divine in that sense; they don't tell me the future. They are a lens through which to attune myself to what I already know. Looking at this spread together, perhaps I need to find a way to restory my experience, reorient myself to the present moment as a means of reorienting myself to the future.

* * *

Friends and family who don't navigate the tricky waters of academia don't understand, which creates a new level of loneliness. I love what I do. But more and more, I'm trying to figure out how to be more than "what I do." This isn't solely an academic problem in our late-stage capitalist world, but it has different dimensions to it.

I'm reckoning with what loneliness means for me, and in contrast, what it means to be content as an academic whose work/life balance will always be blurred.

* * *

I look at the time and pack the cards up. This has been a fun diversion, taken in pursuit of finding a way to end this essay, maybe even give it some poetic balance. I should return to this practice. Carve out more time for self-care and reflection. More and more academics, particularly BIPOC folks, are speaking to practices of collective care and healing that I find deeply important. In her manifesto *Rest Is Resistance*, Tricia Hersey argues for radical rest: "I believe rest, sleep, naps, daydreaming, and slowing down can help us all wake up to see the truth of ourselves. Rest is a healing portal to our deepest selves. Rest is care. Rest is radical" (7). I tell myself to create more space. Perhaps after this next course prep, this next conference presentation, this next service project, this next writing deadline.

Works Cited

Gaiman, Neil. *American Gods*. 10th Anniversary ed., Harper Collins, 2011.
Hersey, Tricia. *Rest Is Resistance: A Manifesto*. Little, Brown Spark, 2022.
Kabat-Zinn, Jon. *Wherever You Go There You Are: Mindfulness Meditation in Everyday Life*. 10th ed., Hachette, 2005.
Penrose, Lysa. "Cozy Wisdoms: 8 Tarot Spreads for Magical Living." Self-published, n.d.

To the Fringes and Back
Academic Life in the Rural Midwest

CAMILO PERALTA

As a first-generation college student, I have had more than my share of challenges navigating the murky and often perilous waters of academia. I wish I'd had mentors or a little guidance somewhere along the way, but I never got involved much as an undergraduate—it took me a few years just to figure out what I wanted to major in. Even after settling on English, I found it difficult to make friends or connect with my professors. The more-than-hour-long commute from my parents' house by Chicago's O'Hare to Loyola's main campus on the lakeshore probably didn't help matters, either.

Indeed, the best advice I ever received about higher ed probably came from an unlikely source: my father, who only made it through six years of formal schooling back in Guatemala. "Son," he used to say, "if you're going to major in something as useless as English literature, you'd better get yourself a graduate degree. Otherwise, prepare to be the first college grad working the fryer at McDonald's." *How could he possibly know anything about that?* I'd scoff, with all the arrogance and optimism of youth. Then I graduated, and discovered just how right he was about the bleak job market for English B.A.s.

I spent the next two decades bouncing around between jobs of varying tolerability. I taught English overseas, waited a table or two, and suffered through a painful stint in pharmacy retail that lasted far longer than I care to admit. By the time I decided to heed pop's advice about pursuing a graduate degree, I was in my early 30s, managing inventory at a printing company and living in a tiny studio apartment in the northern suburbs of Chicago.

Going back to school, even as a fully online student, re-invigorated me. I had always loved reading and writing about literature, but for the first time, I began to realize that those were things I could actually get paid to do. Maybe not handsomely, but as someone earning minimum wage in one of the most expensive cities in the country, I couldn't imagine that it could get much worse, financially. I started applying for jobs before my last term, and counted myself lucky to land a few interviews during the critical summer between the conferral of my degree and the start of the fall semester. One of those interviews turned into a job offer, which I accepted despite the fact that it was a temporary position in a part of the country I had little interest in visiting, let alone staying in for any length of time.

Three states, four institutions, and eight years later, I have taken up my latest teaching position, at a community college right outside of my hometown. It is tenure track, well-paid, and union-protected. Best of all, we're only an hour away from family, which is especially important to us now that we have a new addition to the family. It feels as if I have come full circle, and though I know that I wouldn't have made it even to the first round of interviews for this job without all of that experience, I can't help but think that I might have gotten here a little sooner, if I'd had some help somewhere along the way.

I still don't know much about academia, let alone what it is like to teach at Ivy League or R1 institutions ... but when it comes to small, rural colleges and universities in the middle of nowhere, I suppose I am about as much of an expert as they come. The following reflection on these experiences is offered for any aspiring English professors who might find themselves undertaking a similar journey through the rural fringes of academia. I hope it can help someone avoid some of the mistakes I've made ... starting, perhaps, with my decision to accept the very first position that was offered to me during that initial job hunt in the spring and summer of 2016.

Oklahoma!

My year at Southwestern Oklahoma State University had its share of good and bad. The town itself resembled so many of the others I would come to call home in the next few years: quiet, isolated, population of 10,000 people, almost entirely Caucasian. Everyone dressed like a cowboy, though I could never quite bring myself to adopt the local fashion sense. It was in Weatherford that I first got used to the long drives along wide, empty highways that are a distinguishing feature of life in the rural Midwest. But the bright lights and surprisingly diverse food scene of Oklahoma City were only an hour away, and we could reach bustling Yukon in even less time than that. In truth, I was too busy drawing up lesson plans for my developmental writing classes to have much time for fun.

I suppose the English Department at SWOSU must resemble its

counterparts at larger, urban institutions in certain ways, but it was also the kind of place that could only really exist in Western Oklahoma. There was a fedora-wearing poet who lent me a massive binder containing his entire life's work, which he demanded back only a week later. The sanctimonious lit professor who insisted that comic books and video games were as culturally significant as the works of Homer or Shakespeare. (I enjoy the odd superhero movie or round of *Civilization* as much as the next person, but come on!) Most of the department consisted of East Coast transplants who resented having to live in Oklahoma and made no pretense of harboring any scholarly or even pedagogical ambition. They seemed content to pass the time until their inevitable retirements bickering about obscure subjects during interminably long department meetings.

I was in Weatherford when Trump won the 2016 election. Several of my colleagues canceled classes in solidarity (so they said) with their emotionally distraught, even traumatized, students, though I didn't notice any discernible change in my own classes. One of the oddest features of academic life on the fringes must be the contrast between the often-radical progressivism that prevails on most college campuses and the more traditional values of the rural communities in which they are located. Watching my colleagues go into repeated hysterics in the weeks and months following Trump's election, I couldn't help but wonder why they would choose to settle down in a place where they were sure to have strong disagreements with the political and social views of their neighbors.

I made one friend while I was there, a prominent scholar of Jane Austen and popular culture with multiple publications to his name, including several books. Predictably, he was employed by the mediocrities who ran the place as a part-time adjunct. He was originally from New York; like me, a stranger in a strange land, which perhaps explains why we became friends. The year after I left, he was finally granted a full-time position, and claims to be happy there, though he has since shifted his research interests from comic books to African American literature, and now writes autobiographical fiction in a quixotic attempt to attract interest in his work.

I had signed a one year, renewable contract. Given my indifferent relations with the rest of the department and lack of enthusiasm for the position, I was neither surprised nor disappointed not to be invited back for another round. I had already decided that one year was enough, especially at the paltry salary ($38,000 per year, with a 30-credit class load, or five writing-intensive classes in both the fall and spring terms). I notice with not a little satisfaction that, every year since I left, the school has advertised the same, temporary position I had taken as a newly minted MA. It comforts me to know that I am not alone in viewing it as a stepping stone to other, hopefully greater, things.

Kansas

That wasn't quite the case, however, with my next job, which was located four hours north, across the border in southeast Kansas. Without question, one of the most challenging aspects of living and working in rural places is the difficulty of getting around. Whether driving home for the holidays or flying across the country for a conference presentation, there is often no easy way of getting from point A to B. "Going home for the holidays" often entails some difficult choices: should we find someone to take care of the cat for the week and fly back to Chicago, or spend several days driving there and back? Or was it best to call off the whole thing altogether? Of all the inconveniences and minor irritations of this career, surely none is as painful as having to spend long periods of time far away from loved ones and family.

Less serious, but even more frustrating, perhaps, is the lack of dining options in so many rural college towns. Weatherford at least had a cheap buffet; in Independence, Kansas, population 10,000 and shrinking every year, the restaurant scene was absolutely dire. The interview committee took me to what was then the finest restaurant in town (since closed) ... when I visited again a few months later with my wife, we ate at what must have surely been the worst Chinese buffet in all of Kansas (also closed now). We spent the next two years cooking at home, mostly, and occasionally venturing out to a local steakhouse that wasn't too expensive but always seemed half-empty. (They closed about a month after we left.) On the rare occasions when my wife would agree to fast food, we had to choose between Braum's, McDonald's, and Taco Bell. Like most Midwestern towns, Indy has its share of Mexican restaurants, run by kind and hard-working locals. But to someone who grew up in Chicago, the microwaved fare they serve at these places just doesn't cut it.

Aside from the food, I actually liked living in Independence. It has its own stubborn and idiosyncratic character that sets it apart from the Weatherfords of the world. Local celebrities include William Inge, an excellent and overlooked playwright, Laura Ingalls Wilder, who spent some time there as a child, and Miss Able, one of the first monkeys sent into outer space. Apparently, it was at one time home to more millionaires per capita than any other place in the U.S., a fact the locals still like to boast about, although the millionaires left long ago, leaving their mansions to ruin all across town. Abandoned properties from less prosperous former residents dot the neighborhoods and central business district; consequently, land is very cheap in Indy. One of my neighbors had a sign tacked to the back of his garage offering his run-down property for $33,000, and that was by no means a rare sight.

However much I enjoyed living there, teaching at Independence Community College was a horrible, soul-crushing experience—looking back on it now, I cannot believe I lasted as long as two years. I should have known things were not all they seemed when I showed up on the first day of the fall semester and noticed that each of my classes seemed to be packed to the brim with athletes. I have nothing against college athletes, the vast majority of whom are hard-working, diligent students, but these were of a different sort. I soon learned the reason why: Independence would be playing host to the next season of the popular Netflix show, *Last Chance U*, which focuses on college athletes who are forced to attend low-ranked schools due to poor grades or behavior. Rather than the local track or football stars one might expect, most of the athletes in my classes were inner-city youth far from Kansas, who had little desire to be there and even less interest in their education.

At a stronger institution, surrounded by more capable students, they might have been okay. But the administrators at Indy had decided to sacrifice everything for the sake of gridiron glory, and everyone knew it. The athletics department treated class as baby-sitting for the athletes, and forced them to attend every day. So you couldn't just kick them out if they were disruptive, or remind them that they didn't need to be there.

Things got even worse in Year 2. Students who formerly could be tricked or cajoled into cooperating muttered and even swore at me openly in the classroom. At the start of the spring term, two massive football players came to my office one day and began shouting at me because I had dared to give them a failing grade for an obvious case of plagiarism. I genuinely felt unsafe reporting to work after that, though I did so, anyway, after a few days off for unspecified "mental health reasons." Rather than being expelled, the illiterate delinquents were forced to issue a half-hearted apology, and then allowed to drop the class quietly.

By then, I had a few job interviews lined up. I couldn't afford to be particular about where we ended up, because I knew that I would rather go back to that printing job in Chicago than spend another year at ICC. When I was invited to interview at a public university across the state in northwest Kansas, I jumped at the opportunity to escape Indy. There are dream jobs, and there are jobs you take in the hopes that something better will someday come along.... I accepted my next position, at Fort Hays State University, knowing that it would probably prove the latter.

The English department at Fort Hays State University reminded me of the one at SWOSU in some ways, but my colleagues were much nicer, including my new chair, who would go out of his way over the next few years to treat me like regular faculty. It was another NTT, renewable position, but my full load consisted of only four classes per term, instead of five. It paid a little better than either SWOSU or ICC, but the biggest advantage, for me, was the chance to work with a friendly and engaged student body. No more overgrown man-children chasing impossible dreams. FHSU is the only four-year school west of Salina, and attracts students from all of the farms, ranches, and small towns throughout western Kansas. Lots of career-focused majors eager to escape their modest upbringings, with just enough literary-minded types to keep a small department in English going.

Covid hit in the spring of my first year there. We got an email one day announcing the abrupt transition to online classes. That would last until the end of the term; in the fall, we were given the option of teaching totally online or trying out the brand-new and rather ominous-sounding "hybrid" modality. Since my wife and I were trying for a baby, I chose the former, and got lots of practice talking to a screen full of black boxes. Outside of campus, the city of Hays implemented a requirement to mask in public spaces, which was inconsistently observed and abandoned after about a month. In general, Covid was never a big deal in western Kansas, and things were back to normal within a year of the initial outbreak.

In hindsight, a town like Hays might be the ideal place to spend a pandemic. There's isolated and rural, and then there's isolated and rural *in Western Kansas* ... the two are not exactly the same. Weatherford, as I have noted, was about 45 minutes away from the suburbs of Oklahoma City, and you could get to Tulsa or Joplin in twice that time from Independence. In Hays, however, you were looking at a 90 minute drive even to middling Salina; the hospitals and airports of Wichita were another hour away. Denver and Kansas City were a grim and lonely five hour ride along either direction of I-80. My students and colleagues assured me that long drives were just something you get used to, but as someone who doesn't like driving to begin with, it was probably one of my least favorite things about living in Hays.

Nevertheless, I spent four productive and happy years at FHSU, and I shall always be grateful to my former colleagues there for saving me from ICC. I was treated well, given the chance to teach a wide variety of classes, and supported in my research endeavors. I made another lifelong friend, Morgan Chalfant, a poet and writer of Gothic fiction with an unfortunate addiction to energy drinks. (I left him the small cooler I bought to keep my drinks cool while they were renovating the department breakroom.) During my fourth and final year there, my wife and I learned that we were expecting a baby, who was born in March of 2023. I look forward to bringing Julia back to Hays someday so that she can see the charming little town in which she was born.

Back to Chicago

A few days after the birth of my daughter, we received more good news: a job offer from Joliet Junior College, the first and oldest community college in the country. Though sad to leave our home of the past four years, my wife and I were excited about getting to raise Julia in a more familiar environment, and closer to our family in Chicago. We sold off most of the furniture we'd accumulated, packed up the old Yaris, and headed out once again on the long, cross-country drive. Except for Cho the cat, who doesn't much care for being in a car, all of us felt rejuvenated at the thought of the fresh start that awaited us.

One year later, I'm convinced that this decision was the correct one. JJC offers many of the same benefits I'd enjoyed at my previous institutions, with few or none of the downsides. In fact, the only example of the latter I can think of is the much longer commute: in Oklahoma and Kansas, I never had to drive more than five minutes to campus each morning, but now spend at least an hour of each workday sitting in a car. I consider that an acceptable trade-off for the higher pay and greater job security I enjoy here. Besides, I only have to be on campus four days a week.

Now a tenure-track associate professor with eight years of teaching experience under my belt, I still don't claim to be any kind of expert about academia. And, having spent so much of my adult life outside of it, I doubt that will ever change, or that it really matters. I have finally found a job I can see myself doing until the day I retire, and couldn't ask for more. If I have any advice to offer, it is directed at nervous humanities and English graduates who don't know where else to get it from, other than their parents ... as well as anyone dissatisfied with their current position or struggling to make it as an adjunct. Remember that there is more to higher education than the Ivy League, and that many fine institutions exist outside of large urban areas on either coast. Don't be afraid to explore opportunities wherever they may arise, even if they lead you to the rural fringes of academia, to towns and states you never knew existed and can't imagine yourself living in. Who knows? You may discover a taste for that kind of lifestyle, as I did. Just be careful to avoid the many hazards that lie in wait there. And whatever you do, if you hear that your employers will be featured on a reality television program: *run!*

Becoming an Academic in Japan
Negotiating Age, Gender and Nationality

SUZANNE KAMATA

When my Japanese husband and I were awaiting the birth of our twins, I fully expected to take a few months off, and then resume teaching English as a Foreign Language in Tokushima, Japan, where we lived. Furthermore, I expected that I would be able to obtain a full-time university teaching position like several of my foreign peers who had, like me, arrived in the country in the late 1980s and early 1990s, during Japan's "bubble economy." I did not anticipate, however, that my daughter's disabilities would delay my re-entry into the workforce, and that an economic downturn, a declining population, and persistent discrimination due to age, nationality, and gender would become potentially insurmountable barriers. In this essay, I discuss some of the challenges that I faced attempting to forge a career as an academic as the middle-aged foreign mother of a daughter with disabilities in Japan.

Learning to Teach

I came of age in the United States in the 1980s, after the second wave of feminism, with the assumption that I would get a college degree and have a career. My first job after graduation was as an Assistant English Teacher in Japan as part of the then-fledgling Japanese government–sponsored Japan Exchange and Teaching (JET) Program. I was assigned to a high school, where I helped out in classes by reading textbook passages out loud, and by giving students a chance to practice their conversational skills in English. I sometimes asked the students about their future ambitions, and I was surprised by how many times high school girls told me that they aspired to be good wives and mothers. Perhaps like many young Japanese women, they would go on to college, and perhaps travel or work for a bit. Meanwhile, I knew women my age back home who were embarking on careers as dentists, engineers, and accountants.

I did not initially aspire to become an academic. When I graduated from the University of South Carolina in 1987 with a bachelor's degree in English, I had dreamed of becoming a novelist. I would travel the world by teaching abroad in various countries and gather material for my books. Eventually, I would settle back in the United States, my native country. As it turned out, during my second year in the teaching program, I met and fell in love with the Japanese physical education teacher who would become my husband.

The JET Program, which was actually conceived of as more of a diplomatic exchange than a language teaching scheme, had a two-year limit. In theory, young native speakers were expected to return to their respective home countries and report upon the charms of Japan. As my husband-to-be was reluctant to leave Japan, I had to find another job in order to secure a visa and continue living in the country. Luckily, the Japanese economy was strong, as was the desire of many Japanese to improve their English-language ability. Thanks to a change in Japanese law, public schools were beginning to hire foreigners on yearly renewable contracts as "foreign language specialists." I easily found a new job working at the Board of Education in a neighboring town. My job was primarily to teach English to students at two of the elementary schools. Up to forty students were in each class, which sometimes made discipline a challenge. Additionally, I was expected to teach adult learners of different levels in the evening, and a class called "Mother/Child English Conversation." In retrospect, I had a challenging schedule, but I was making more money than I would have in the States, and I was learning how to be a teacher. I expected to eventually transition into university teaching. In the late 1980s, it was possible to get an academic job in Japan with nothing but a bachelor's degree and a native accent.

Taking Time Off for Motherhood

After five years of marriage, I became pregnant with twins at the age of thirty-three. According to my contract, I was entitled to six weeks' leave before birth, and eight weeks of maternity leave. I expected that these fourteen weeks would give me enough time to arrange for childcare, and that I would be able to continue working. (Japanese public servants are allowed three years of partially paid leave; however, since I was on a one-year contract, I was not entitled to an extended leave.) Although I wanted to spend time at home while my children were small, I knew that our family would struggle on just my high school teacher husband's income. I felt that I needed to contribute to our finances.

When my twins were born fourteen weeks prematurely, I suddenly lost my six weeks' prenatal leave. My son and daughter remained in the hospital's NICU for three and four months, respectively. Returning to work at that time was unthinkable, and so I was forced to quit my job. Later, we discovered that our daughter had cerebral palsy and was deaf, which created further complications. Although my employers were willing to take me back, my babies required special care. Due to their delicate immune systems, they could not be put into preschools. For my babies, a common cold could—and later did—turn into a life-threatening illness. My ageing mother-in-law was both resistant to, and probably incapable of, looking after infant twins on her own. I was also reluctant to ask her because our culturally informed ideas about child-raising were very different. Early on, we had arguments over whether to give babies honey, and when to begin potty training. Additionally, my daughter was in an early intervention program at the public School for the Deaf. In order to develop the skills to communicate with her, I was expected to attend as well. The school urged working mothers to quit their jobs and devote themselves to their children's development and care. Unlike in the U.S. where there seems to be a continuous discussion on whether it is better to be a stay-at-home mother or a working mother, in Japan, quitting one's job or taking time off to raise children was not only expected, but honorable.

While my daughter was still in preschool, I was offered a full-time teaching position at a public college for teachers on the basis of my first published book, *The Broken Bridge: Fiction from Expatriates in Literary Japan*, an anthology which I had edited before the birth of my children. I did not yet have an advanced degree. The job was attractive, but I felt that it was important to spend time with my daughter to make sure that she developed communication skills, and that I learned to communicate with her. If I had placed her in a public daycare facility, she would not have had the specialized care that she needed. I regretfully declined the position, but I assumed that in a year or two another well-paying job in academia would turn up.

Entering Academia in Middle Age

When my daughter entered elementary school, I was no longer expected to stay at school all day. I still had to drive her to and from school, but I had enough free time during the day to fit in a few part-time lessons.

Through a friend, I learned of an upcoming opening for a part-time instructor at the teacher's college. I applied for the position and was hired. Thus, I entered academia as an adjunct.

A year later I was hired to teach two additional classes at a private university after a friend recommended me to her department chair. I was also hired to teach a class at the largest public university in the prefecture; therefore, I was employed at three separate institutions, all within easy driving distance from our home. At the time, I felt it was an ideal situation. I was earning a significant amount of money working a few hours a day, while being able to bring my children to school and pick them up. Additionally, teaching at universities gave me more prestige than teaching in elementary schools had afforded me. Meanwhile, I continued to read and write, ultimately publishing numerous stories, articles, reviews, and essays, plus four books related to my experiences as a mother. I had also become Fiction Editor of Literary Mama, an online literary journal devoted to writing about motherhood, and I was invited to give a speech at the private university where I taught on the conflict between working mothers and stay-at-home mothers in the United States.

By the time my children were in junior high school, and no longer so much in need of my attention, I was ready to work full-time. Unfortunately, finding a well-paying job was no longer easy. Japan's economic bubble had burst. Hourly wages for private English teachers had dropped. Even salaries for civil servants, my husband's included, had gone down. Due to the economic downturn, changes in university policies, and a decrease in population, the teaching job market had tightened considerably.

Around this time, an Australian friend who was also teaching as an adjunct with a partially completed master's degree suddenly became the sole breadwinner for her family when her husband, a Japanese doctor, was diagnosed with cancer. She was unable to find permanent, full-time employment, and began making plans to return to her home country. I realized that if something similar happened to me, I would have a hard time getting a job in academia in the United States with only a bachelor's degree. Also, I knew that I now needed at least a master's degree in order to secure employment as a lecturer at a Japanese university. Considering that an MFA is a terminal degree, I applied and was accepted into the Optional Residency MFA in Creative Writing Program at the University of British Columbia in Canada.

I was now forty-eight years old. I had heard rumors that it was next to impossible to get a full-time university job after fifty, so time was of the essence. Although there are now laws against age and gender discrimination in Japan (and elsewhere), when I first arrived, the employment ads in *The Japan Times* frequently specified age ranges. One ad for a new English language magazine read, "Applicants, male or female, aged from twenty-two to about thirty-five, must be proficient in English, but no experience is required." This is no doubt partly because younger energetic teachers are seen as more attractive, and partly because age is often a factor when determining salary. At public universities in Japan, it is generally cheaper to hire a thirty-year-old than a fifty-year-old.

In addition, Japanese labor laws discourage women from working outside the home. Husbands are allowed a tax break if their working wives make less than 1.03 million yen per year (approximately $6,500). This was part of a governmental strategy to increase the dwindling population; however, making women stay home has not led to more babies. In spite of Japan's shrinking labor force, there is little financial incentive for women in this country to go back to work full time after their childbearing years are over. Perhaps my own expectations were unrealistic in this conservative corner of Japan. Nevertheless, I felt that I had earned my due. I had now acquired eight years of university teaching experience, as well as significant publications.

The Pursuit of Full-Time Employment

When I was a year into my graduate program, full-time positions opened at three area colleges. Two were at the public universities where I was already teaching part-time, and another was at a private, family-owned university. I decided to apply to all three. I was invited to an interview at the private university. My interrogators were nine men around the age of sixty. Although each one asked me a question, the "interview" was more of a conversation than an actual job interview. One man told me that he was my husband's occasional drinking buddy, and that they had plans to go out together the following week. (I later learned that he had been the principal at the school where my husband had taught, and also his mentor.) I could not help thinking that the comment was unprofessional. What did my husband have to do with my university teaching career?

Later that evening, my husband's friend called him—not me—and congratulated him on my success. It seemed that I would be offered the job. I had been planning on attempting to negotiate contract details once I was officially offered employment. However, the university sent me a contract in the mail and asked me to sign it and send it back. The salary offered was the same as that which I had received as a twenty-two-year-old, newly landed in Japan on the JET Program—slightly less than had been advertised, with additional work teaching kindergarten children attached. I felt that I deserved better and told them so, but the university said, "Take it or leave it." I left it. A German acquaintance who taught full time at the large public university, and whose Japanese wife taught part-time at the same institution, told me that I should have taken the sure thing, and that it would have been a decent "second income." I felt I deserved more.

An American man, another acquaintance, was ultimately hired for the position. He was single and had been working continuously as an Assistant English Teacher in a public junior high school. He had completed a master's degree, but he had no publications or college-level teaching experience. Nevertheless, he was asked to declare his most recent salary, with the understanding that he would receive more in his new position.

Perhaps it is typical for employers to assume that a woman returning to work after a long absence is rusty, and has to relearn skills. I was resentful, however, of their condescension. After all, I had been teaching at the university level for eight years, and I had more publications than many tenured Japanese university instructors. I cannot say whether or not I would have been offered a higher salary if I had already been working full-time, but I do know that women in academia in Japan face an uphill battle. The careers of women in higher education tend to lag behind their male counterparts because they have fewer opportunities to develop their careers due to constraints placed upon them by their families, and also because of power and sexual harassment. Due to my daughter's disabilities, I had taken even more time off than usual.

Around this time, John, an instructor at the large public university, sent me a private email message, unbidden, telling me that the second job that I had applied for was "earmarked for another colleague." I understood that he was trying to help his friend, a male part-time teacher, get a job. This man was an American married to a Japanese woman, with a small child. I figured he was trying to make things easy for his friend, the principal earner in his family, by shooing me out of the way. I also recognized that I was experiencing power harassment for the first time, and that it was coming not from a Japanese man, but from a fellow American.

Many Western men adopt Japanese gendered bias after settling here. Or perhaps Japanese attitudes free them to express secretly held beliefs. When I recently commented upon the tidiness of a male Canadian instructor's office, he confessed that one of his female students had offered to clean it. Of course, he had accepted. I cannot imagine a serious female American student offering to clean her instructor's room. Although I had no hard evidence, I couldn't help thinking that my male would-be colleagues looked upon me in the same way—a woman, looking to supplement her husband's income.

Many of the foreign men I knew were married to Japanese women who did not have full-time jobs. But I also knew several foreign women married to Japanese men who were the main wage earners in their families. In any case, I informed the university that an instructor had tried to dissuade me from submitting an application. He was reprimanded, and I was ultimately hired for the job, with a one-year contract, renewable for three years.

A Three-Year Contract

My office was in a building largely devoted to science. There was a lab downstairs, where students in white coats and goggles gathered to study, and another room from which white clouds gusted whenever the door was opened. Although there were several English instructors in the Department of Integrated Arts and Sciences, I was the only English instructor in the General Education department, and the only foreigner. I was also one of only two women. The other was a friendly Japanese professor of psychology who smiled at me from across the room during our monthly obligatory faculty meetings. My boss's office was next to mine, but he was almost never in it and rarely responded to email. I understood that I was on my own.

On that first day, I pocketed the key and went to my new office. The floor was scuffed and there were old books on the shelves from previous occupants. A brand new computer, still in its box, sat on the desk. I had no idea of how to hook it up, or whom to ask. Another colleague suggested I get one of the students who was on the staff of the English Support Room to set it up, and that is what I did.

Over the following semester, I taught seven ninety-minute classes per week, managed a staff of ten students and part-time instructors who held English chat sessions and special workshops in the English Support Room, and attended faculty meetings. I was also a full-time graduate student, and was preparing to publish a new novel. Although I had not been hired as a researcher, I knew that the university valued refereed academic publications, so I began to write a paper.

I was happy then. I had an office, with my books on the shelves, a coffee maker, and a carpet that I had bought at Ikea to cover the scuff marks. For once, I could travel to writers' conferences without depleting our family's budget. "Once you're in, you're in," my tenured friend told me. Universities in remote areas, such as where we lived, sometimes have a difficult time attracting quality candidates, and hiring committees would often rather deal with someone familiar than the unknown. Although many instructors had been initially hired on fixed contracts, my friend did not know of anyone who had ever left. Typically, past employees' contracts had been quietly renewed, or they had been eased into other positions.

At the beginning of my second year on the job, a tenured position was advertised. My boss, the dean, strongly encouraged me to apply for it, even calling me at home on the weekend to see how my application was coming along. I had some questions about formatting, so I dropped in on a foreign colleague, also in a contract position, whose Japanese literacy exceeded mine. He seemed surprised by the job announcement.

"This isn't for you," he said. "I think this is for John."

I told him that I was being pressured to apply, and that I was under the impression that the job had been designed for me. Once again, there was a very short window of opportunity—applications would only be accepted over a period of ten days, and the job would begin mid-semester. I submitted my application, and then was asked to resubmit, after the deadline had passed, when it turned out that I had used the wrong forms.

Time passed. Nothing happened. The job was reposted, with different requirements. A month or so later, the foreign colleague announced on Facebook that he had been hired for the position, and then he blocked me from Facebook, deleted a five-star review of my latest novel from Amazon.com, and stopped coming to my office. In fact, he never spoke to me again. Confused, I sent him a call for papers related to his field of studies. He replied with a curt "I already knew about it. But thanks." During a meeting that we both attended, me as an "observer," I ventured a simple question. The foreign colleague turned to the chairman of the meeting and said, "She's not supposed to speak, is she?" Later, when I submitted a women's studies paper to the in-house journal, he was chosen as the sole "referee" and ripped my paper to shreds, questioning my intelligence. It seems that I had made an enemy, but I was not sure how. I did my best to avoid him.

Although I felt that I had grounds for a complaint against this colleague, I did not want to make waves. His behavior was petty and if I brought it to the attention of my superiors here in Japan where harmony is highly valued, our conflict might be seen as a foreigners' problem. Microaggression is by no means limited to Westerners, and is quite common in Japan, but any troubles among foreign staff members might reinforce Japanese stereotypes about immigrants. I thought it was better to continue to teach diligently, engage in research, and publish and present at conferences.

In retrospect, perhaps having been rendered meek by the mothers at my daughter's school during my off-time from employment, I was fundamentally unfit to deal with faculty incivility endemic to an institution striving to increase its prestige. As the mother of a disabled child, I had

had to learn to be tolerant and patient, but I felt vulnerable. I was now the only woman in my department. Motherhood had been the focus of much of my writing, and I knew that it was important, but I suddenly worried that my conservative Japanese male colleagues might discount my topic as overly domestic. Furthermore, one Saturday, while I was visiting a museum with my daughter, I ran into the head of my department, a sixtyish Japanese man. I briefly introduced him to my daughter using sign language, but I had a flash of worry that after seeing me pushing my daughter in her wheelchair, he might come to the conclusion, even subconsciously, that I should be at home, attending to her needs, not at the university.

During my third year, the university declared a hiring freeze. Nevertheless, a special three-year non-renewable position was created and advertised, calling for a Native English instructor with writing expertise, Teaching English as a Foreign Language (TEFL) and curriculum development experience. According to the ad, which was not in English, Japanese language skills were not required. I applied for and was invited to interview for the position. I felt confident about my application. By this time I had racked up some peer-reviewed academic publications, presented at international conferences (sometimes with my daughter in tow), and I had won prestigious awards for my novel about a teenager with cerebral palsy and for a nonfiction manuscript about traveling with my disabled daughter. I had also taught many large classes, helped with university entrance exams, conducted research with university colleagues, voluntarily conducted writing workshops for students and faculty, and hosted an international writing conference. I believed that all of these things made me an attractive candidate.

Failure to Thrive

My foreign colleague was one of five on the hiring committee. At the beginning of our interview, he rattled some papers and pointed out a mistake that I had made in Japanese on my resume, and then argued that I was sloppy and unreliable. "This isn't a job where you can just leave at five o'clock," he sneered. I recalled then that he had once seen me leaving campus early to pick up my daughter from school; however, this had not interfered with my duties.

Another professor on the all-male hiring committee asked, "Sure, you have all of these publications and awards, but what about your teaching?" Another, the one who had seen me pushing my daughter's wheelchair at the museum, asked, "If you are not hired for this position, would you be willing to continue teaching the classes that you have been scheduled for on a part-time basis?"

Ultimately, the job went to the one other person who had been interviewed—a younger, ambitious, child-free American woman whose husband was already a tenured Associate Professor at the university. Although she had fewer publications than I had, she had previously taught full-time on a limited contract at another university in another part of Japan. She and her husband had been invited to dinner at the house of the professor on the hiring committee who had been unimpressed by my awards and publications.

I assumed that my academic career was over. I applied for unemployment benefits. One of the stipulations for receiving money was that I had to apply for a new job. While, at the time, there were no full-time academic jobs available in the prefecture where we lived, I came across a number of postings in Kyoto, where my daughter would be entering a group home for the deaf. Although the city was two and a half hours from our home, I could rent a small apartment if I got a job there, and visit my husband on the occasional weekend. I applied for a full-time position teaching English Language courses at a university in Kyoto, and was called for an interview. When I arrived, I saw that I was only one of two women, out of about twenty applicants, being interviewed for twelve available positions. Since many universities are actually making an effort to hire more women and correct the gender imbalance, I realized that my chances were good. Ultimately, I was offered a five-year-contract position.

Around the time that I received the paperwork for this position, I was suddenly approached about a full-time tenured job closer to home. I, the known quantity, was being asked if I would like to replace a foreign English instructor at one of the colleges where I had been teaching part-time. Happy ending: I said "yes."

Academic Freedom in Erdogan's Turkey

Evren Altinkas

The higher education system in Turkey is a multi-layered and complex structure. In 1981, Turkey's higher education system was extensively restructured in accordance with the new Higher Education Law No. 2547. Thus, all higher education institutions were connected to the Council of Higher Education (YÖK) and the system became centralized. After this restructuring, all higher education institutions were designed as universities. Higher education has become widespread throughout the country, application to higher education has been centralized, and a central university examination and placement system has begun to be implemented. In addition to public universities, Turkey's first private non-profit university opened to students in 1986.

Academics who have completed their doctoral education become Doctor Lecturer, which is equivalent to the position of tenure-track Assistant Professor in North America. Doctor Lecturers have a difficult process to go through in order to be appointed to the positions of Associate Professor and Professor. Associate Professor evaluations are carried out by an institution called the Interuniversity Board Presidency (ÜAK) in Turkey. Associate Professor candidates apply by uploading their works to the Associate Professorship Application System (DBS), and these works are examined using a point system by the jury members (Professors from different universities) determined by UAK. To qualify for Associate Professorship, candidates must accumulate at least 100 points from various activities, with at least 90 of these points earned after receiving their Ph.D., and earn a score of at least 55 out of 100 on any foreign language exam.

After graduating from a public university in Turkey, I was immediately employed as a Teaching/Graduate Assistant at the same department in 1998. I received a fellowship, and studied at King's College, London for my Master's degree. After that, I returned to Turkey and continued with a second Master's degree and a Ph.D. while I was still employed in the same position and at the same department until 2012. When I was a graduate student employed to do research and teach in Turkey, the challenges I faced as a student of history and political science made me think about the country's intellectual tradition. One of these challenges was the lack of independent academic resources in libraries and in the curriculum offered by graduate programs. Most of the readings and resources available in universities and research institutions were either produced by official government entities or offered no challenges to those official views. It was quite interesting to see how universities were transformed into essentially advanced high schools after the 1980 military coup. Approximately 100 academic personnel were dismissed from universities following the coup due to their alleged leftist political tendencies and were replaced with unqualified high school and night school teachers.

These newly appointed teachers were granted the title "Assistant Professor" overnight, even though they did not hold doctoral degrees. They became the new deans, department chairs and professors at the regime's universities. During my academic career as a graduate student, I had a chance to meet some of them in seminars, talks and conferences. This experience made me think about the origins of the intellectual tradition in Turkey and I decided to write my Ph.D. dissertation on intellectuals in the late Ottoman state and early Turkish Republic. I have compared the development of intellectuals in this period with the development of intellectual strata in Britain, France and Germany. My research showed that the lack of intellectual capacity and critical thinking in most Turkish universities can be traced to post–1950 intellectual traditions, which is the year when the founding political party of the Republic of Turkey became the opposition for the first time since 1923.

Finally, I was hired at a public university in Turkey as a Doctor Lecturer in March 2013. I was on a tenure track, with a path to lifelong job security, as the laws in Turkey stated. I built the whole curriculum along with two of my colleagues for the newly established Department of Political Science at the public university, which was located near the northern border with Georgia. Teaching four classes per semester, actively participating in faculty and Senate meetings, advising students, taking part in hiring committees, and organizing a few international conferences were among my duties.

A few months after my hiring, a series of protests erupted against the Turkish government in May 2013, initially sparked by the government's plan to demolish Istanbul's Gezi Park to make way for a commercial development. This local issue quickly escalated into a broader movement addressing a variety of grievances, including opposition to perceived authoritarianism and the erosion of democratic freedoms under Prime Minister Erdogan's government. Protesters also expressed concerns over issues such as freedom of the press, freedom of expression, and secularism, as well as broader environmental and urban development policies. The heavy-handed police response to the initial protests further fueled public outrage and drew even larger crowds into the streets.

The Gezi protests represented a milestone in the history of Turkish civic life, as participation in these protests was the highest since the establishment of the Republic of Turkey in 1923. According to a report published by the International Federation for Human Rights (FIDH) in April 2014, a total of 5,532 protests were held, with more than 3.6 million people participating between 28 May and 3 September 2013. Some academic personnel joined the protests and/or used their social media accounts to show their support. Other academics wrote online articles and opinion pieces and gave interviews to newspapers, online journals, and news websites.

Being an academic at a public university in Turkey during the Gezi protests in 2013, while actively criticizing government policies, was a challenging and precarious experience. The atmosphere was charged with tension and uncertainty, especially for one teaching sensitive subjects like "Introduction to Political Science" such as myself. As the protests swelled and captured national and international attention, the classroom became an arena for exploring fundamental democratic principles, including the right to protest.

In my lectures, I emphasized that one of the cornerstones of a functioning democracy is the protection of civil liberties, including the right to assemble and express dissent. Drawing parallels between theoretical frameworks and the unfolding events outside, I encouraged students to critically engage with the material and reflect on its real-world implications. This approach, however, did not sit well with the university administration, which was under considerable pressure from the government to maintain a narrative of stability and control.

The tension between my duties as an educator and the expectations placed upon me as a civil servant became palpable. As a public university academic, I was theoretically protected by principles of academic freedom, allowing me to teach and research without undue interference. However, the reality during the Gezi Park protests was starkly different. The government's increasing intolerance of dissent extended to academic institutions, transforming spaces of learning into zones of surveillance and self-censorship.

My open criticism of government policies and my support for the protesters' rights led to significant repercussions. Not long after discussing the protests and the right to dissent in my lectures, I was summoned by the university administration. An investigation was launched against me, ostensibly to determine whether my teachings were in line with the university's guidelines and the "duties expected from a civil servant." The investigation was invasive and stressful. Colleagues were interviewed about my conduct, my lectures were scrutinized, and there was an implicit threat of disciplinary action hanging over my head. The administration's stance was clear: any deviation from the expected narrative could be construed as misconduct. This created an environment of fear and compliance, stifling critical thought and academic freedom.

I was subjected to five different administrative proceedings after September 2013. One of these proceedings stated that I had violated the law by acting "in a way inappropriate for a public servant" and included one of my social media posts ("You must realize that the problem is autocratic government!") as evidence. Although I had a chance to defend myself during the proceeding, I received an official warning from the university as a result of it.

This proceeding was followed by others, and eventually the university administration began to use ridiculous methods to cause more problems for me. One of them was to assign me two separate courses to teach in two different campuses approximately 80 miles apart; my first at the first campus ended at 1:30 p.m. and the next one at the other campus began at 1:50 p.m. I appealed to the university administration about this, but they said that they were expecting me to find a way to be present at the second lecture on time, which of course I could not. This resulted in more administrative proceedings against me.

As a result of ongoing harassment, I resigned from my position in July 2014. Similar sorts of systematic but unofficial harassment used by university administrations against academic staff who participated in the Gezi Protests resulted in the resignation of approximately 800 academic personnel from public and private universities in Turkey between September 2013 and December 2014.

As for me, my unemployment persisted until 2018. After the Gezi Park protests, the political climate in Turkey became increasingly repressive, particularly towards those perceived as dissenters. My involvement in the protests and subsequent investigation by my university had marked me as a potential threat in the eyes of many academic institutions. Public universities, heavily influenced by the government, were particularly wary of hiring individuals with a history of political activism. Each application I submitted was met with silence or polite rejections, often without any substantive reason provided. It became clear that my reputation as a critic of the government was a significant barrier to employment.

Private universities, although theoretically more independent, were also reluctant to take on the risk. The fear of government backlash, potential loss of funding, and the increasing politicization of academia created an environment where hiring decisions were often influenced by considerations of political safety rather than academic merit. My expertise in political science, which should have been an asset, was instead viewed as a liability. Institutions were unwilling to bring in someone who might foster critical thinking and dissent, potentially drawing unwanted attention from authorities.

During these years of unemployment, I struggled to maintain my professional identity and continue my research. I engaged in freelance writing and consulting, but these opportunities were sporadic and insufficient to sustain a stable career. The isolation and financial strain were significant, but the most disheartening aspect was the erosion of my ability to contribute meaningfully to academic discourse in Turkey. The country's intellectual environment was becoming increasingly stifled, and my exclusion from it was both a personal and professional loss.

In 2018, a breakthrough came when I learned about the Scholars-at-Risk program, an initiative designed to protect and support academics facing persecution. After a rigorous application process, I was accepted into the program and offered a position at the University of Guelph in Canada. This opportunity was a lifeline, providing not only employment but also a platform to continue my academic work in a supportive and free environment. At the University of Guelph, I found a community that valued academic freedom and encouraged open dialogue. The Scholars-at-Risk program allowed me to resume my research and teaching without fear of political repercussions. I could openly discuss issues related to democracy, human rights, and political activism, drawing from my own experiences to enrich my work and engage with students.

The transition to Canada was not without its challenges. Adapting to a new cultural and academic environment required significant effort, and the distance from Turkey was both physically and emotionally exhausting. However, the support and acceptance I found at the University of Guelph provided a strong foundation. The experience underscored the importance of international solidarity and the role of global academic networks in supporting scholars at risk.

After my initial position as a Visiting Assistant Professor at the University of Guelph ended in 2022, I found myself facing unemployment once again. While this period was challenging, being in Canada provided a crucial sense of security and freedom that allowed me to continue my research and remain engaged in the academic community. Here, I could still access academic resources, collaborate with colleagues, and contribute to scholarly discourse without the fear of political repercussions that had plagued my career in Turkey. The freedom to explore sensitive topics, critique government policies, and engage in meaningful research was invaluable.

However, the uncertainty of unemployment was a stark reminder of the precarious nature of academic careers, especially for those who have faced persecution. The support I received through the Scholars-at-Risk program had been a lifeline, and now, without a permanent position, I needed to navigate the academic job market once more. This experience highlighted the ongoing challenges faced by displaced scholars, who must continuously seek opportunities to sustain their work and livelihood. Despite these challenges, being in a country that upholds academic freedom is of paramount importance. The ability to conduct research and teach without censorship or fear of retribution is fundamental to the advancement of knowledge and the protection of democratic values. My time in Canada reinforced the significance of safeguarding these freedoms and supporting scholars who defend them. Ultimately, the period following the end of my position at the University of Guelph underscored the resilience required to sustain an academic career in exile. It also reaffirmed the critical need for institutional support and global solidarity in protecting academic freedoms and ensuring that scholars can continue their vital work, regardless of their circumstances.

I would like to finish this essay with a story from Turkey. I hope this story will help readers to understand the importance of academic freedom:

> Once upon a time, a herd of oxen lived in a pasture.
> But the lions in the neighbourhood would not leave them alone.
> They attacked this herd almost every day.
> Oxen are not such a wild animal,
> When they gathered together, they could easily fend off the big lions.
> Day after day, the lions grew anxious.
> "I guess it is up to us to leave this pasture," said one of the lions.
> "Where do we go?" they wondered.
> "Just a minute," they heard a voice say.
> The lame lion, the weakest but cunning member of the herd, took the floor.
> "No," he said, "we are not going anywhere.
> Leave this to me, I will take care of it."
> The lame lion went to the oxen with a white flag.
> "Honourable oxen masters," the lame lion began:
> "Today, we came here to apologize to you. Yes, we attacked you many times,
> but you know why? It's because of that yellow ox among you.
> Give it to us and you can get rid of it and we can live in peace!"
> The gray ox withdrew to talk to the other leaders.
> They all agreed to this proposal.
> Only the old spotted ox said "No," but he could not get anyone to listen to him.

> *The poor yellow ox was handed over to the lions.*
> *One ox for the sake of the whole herd.*
> *Indeed, no one attacked the herd for days.*
> *But this is the lion nation, how long will they be patient?*

The story of the herd of oxen and the lions resonates deeply with my experiences in Turkey, where the yellow ox was given away years ago. This early compromise marked the beginning of a relentless erosion of academic freedom, as each subsequent concession weakened our position further. The initial surrender, driven by fear and the false promise of peace, paved the way for increasing demands and growing repression. Today, the academic landscape in Turkey is a shadow of its former self, with critical voices silenced and intellectual freedom severely constrained.

This narrative serves as a stark warning to the academic community in North America. The initial compromises may seem minor, but they set a dangerous precedent. The yellow ox has already been given in subtle ways—through self-censorship, compliance with external pressures, and the prioritization of funding over integrity. However, it is not too late to protect what remains of academic freedom.

North American scholars must remain vigilant and resist further encroachments on their autonomy. They should unite to defend the principles of free inquiry and open discourse. Allowing even small erosions of these freedoms can lead to a weakened intellectual environment and a compromised future. The lesson from Turkey is clear: once the yellow ox is given, the lions will not be satisfied. Protecting academic freedom requires constant vigilance and a collective commitment to uphold the integrity of scholarly pursuits.

Part II
The Long Run

Seeking Grace

University Faculty in a Post-Covid, Anti-CRT, Anti-DEI, Anti-Tenure Environment

Derek Charles Catsam

Disrupting the Disruptors—Shared Governance and Its Discontents in the Modern University

Un- and under-qualified upper-level administrators. Exploding numbers of vice presidents. No faculty merit raises in years but constant administrative growth. Heightened tensions between faculty and administration and administrative traps set to punish vocal faculty members. Faculty being asked to constantly justify their value despite the fact that nearly every dime brought into the institution, through both tuition and state legislative formula funding calculated based on student credit hours, comes directly from the work of faculty. New Handbook of Operating Procedures policies written while bypassing faculty to make punishing faculty easier and challenging those punishments harder. (But the HOP is irrelevant anyway, because administrators ignore it at will—policies exist to bind, but not protect, faculty and to protect, but not bind, administration.) Faculty Senates being ignored while administrators hand pick faculty for committees and claim that those hand-picked faculty members represent "shared governance."

Meanwhile, new administrators who don't grasp academic norms or don't care increasingly are emboldened to violate those norms by punishing tenured faculty for speaking out, for exercising academic freedom or simply freedom of speech. What used to call for a conversation between a faculty member and a Dean to clear the air now results in a vaguely menacing letter in a file. What used to result in heated conversations eventually forgotten now results in retributive downsizing of offices or loss of hard-earned perks. What used to be seen as normal administrative give-and-take results in area coordinators and department chairs being neutered or removed, clearly tying departmental leadership to upper-level administrators and thus continuing the spiral of distrust between faculty and administration.

All of these phenomena represent trends at my university, and probably at yours, especially if you work at a public Masters or Regional Comprehensive university, schools in the second-tier, third-tier, and no-tier in the rankings but that educate the bulk of college and university students, a significant number of graduate students, and a disproportionate number and percentage of poor, working class, and minority students. But at least the football team gets leather chairs embossed with the university mascot at $400 a seat for the 150 seats in their new auditorium reserved just for them, enough to pay a first-year Assistant Professor if we were still in the business of hiring tenure-track faculty. Suffice it to say, for many of us I suspect the H-Net Job Guide has a permanent place in our most readily available tabs, refreshed daily.

And then the pandemic hit. The preceding lamentation reflected the state of things before Covid-19 changed so much in 2020 (and that was the beginning of what was supposed to be a keynote address at a conference on shared governance at the University of Tulsa in the spring of 2020.) But rather than slowing these trends, I think we can argue that the Nova-Coronavirus allowed administrators to do things they had wanted to do all along with the imprimatur of the emergencies that Covid wrought.

Since Covid (and yes, I know for some the past tense implications are problematic, and I respect that perspective) we have had the Christopher Rufo-ization of higher ed, albeit one facilitated by the Gordon Gees of this world. Suddenly DEI (rarely defined), CRT (never defined, certainly never defined and understood accurately—not that accuracy, or honesty, are concerns of its critics), and tenure became targets, alongside books and libraries. The vagueness of many of these attacks was a feature, and not a glitch. Those defending these loathsome acts will say, have said, "No books were banned—name one that the legislation in Florida banned!" The response to this, of course, is that the vagueness is a strength for book banners, because it puts the burden on local librarians to make decisions that can cost them their careers and worse, and it allows the Stormtroopers of "MomsForLiberty" to interpret anything as being objectionable—not just explicit materials, but books about Civil Rights, the Holocaust, and any element of the rights revolution that they see fit, which, with their laser focus on "woke," yet another undefined term, is just about everything.

Grace Asked For: Grace Not Given?

We heard it constantly as faculty during Covid-19. "Please show grace." Show grace to our students (administrators love to pretend they care more about our students than we do). Show grace to staff. Show grace to those administrators who, after all, were just doing what they had to in the environment, even though a lot of what administration felt compelled to do reflected things to ride herd on faculty that they had been wanting to do long before coronavirus.

Amid providing that grace the logical question became, what about grace for us, the faculty, who make a university a university? Covid-19 adjustments have given way to a simulacrum of normalcy yet it appears that grace is further away than ever. This is truer for humanities faculty than any other. Many states, my own perhaps most visibly, are working to eliminate or neuter an already weakened tenure system, with the rhetoric clearly aimed at faculty in fields like History and Literature. Bans on CRT and DEI—again, clearly targeting the humanities—are nothing more than efforts to chill classroom dialogue, dissuade certain research, and intimidate faculty, efforts all the more pernicious because of their ill-defined natures.

To respond to these issues, the University of Texas System's Faculty Advisory Council (UT-SysFAC, or FAC) developed the Covid Legacy Project. The basic principles of the Project were to recognize and affirm that the Covid-19 pandemic, and its aftermath, has had a significant impact on the work faculty, students, and staff do within the University of Texas System, and to develop a long-range plan to ensure that faculty can be successful going forward. We recognize that the impacts of the pandemic will endure years after operations are putatively back to normal and that some of the impacts may linger for years after.

At the heart of this project was this idea of grace: not only to emphasize the grace needed *of* faculty but also to recognize the grace that faculty merit *in return*. It was supported by FAC unanimously, endorsed by the Associate Vice Chancellor for Academic Affairs for the System, and is the one accomplishment that year's FAC Chair said he was proudest of FAC for completing. It is worth pointing out that he is faculty at one of the UT Medical campuses—revealing a unique element to FAC in that it combines academic and medical campuses in what is effectively the UT System Faculty Senate.

Because the one aspect of the pandemic that became part of a larger narrative was that faculty needed to find a way to practice flexibility and show grace—for beleaguered staff, for the person running the remote meeting, for the tough decisions administrators had to make, and especially for our students. And we believe that faculty did this. Indeed, even as administrators, whose interactions are rare and usually shallow, try to use students as a human shield—in effect try to claim that they speak for our students more than we, who see them daily, do—we in fact were the ones who made the adjustments, the accommodations, who showed the flexibility and creativity, who really worked to ensure that our students received a quality, real education, even if we had never taught online before (I am included in that group).

The Covid Legacy Project came up with a list of best practices and added a process to document the impact of Covid on campuses. We then brought this document back to individual campuses—eight academic and five medical campuses—and in theory this is supposed to be implemented as appropriate for each campus. We considered the three traditional legs of the faculty stool. For our purposes here, I'll mention our discussion of teaching. Our basic principle regarding teaching was as follows:

> [T]eaching has experienced disruptions, and innovations in teaching were required to generate curricular renovations and modifications to pivot towards remote and online education. Contributions to high-impact practices such as research, community engagement, and study abroad activities may have been equally delayed. So too has the opportunity for course observation, especially those in face-to-face modalities. Furthermore, these disruptions have had a profound impact on students who may well have taken frustrations with these disruptions out in their only real outlet—teaching evaluations of their faculty. For contingent and junior faculty, professional development opportunities have been severely circumscribed, if not canceled or eliminated. These factors too must be taken into account in assessments of past and future teaching practices.

Specific Project recommendations tended not to focus on any one aspect of the three-legged stool, though naturally, where they did, research limitations and their impact on tenure were often foremost in peoples' minds. But teaching fits into so many of the best practices we developed—mindfulness about the oftentimes dubious nature of student evaluations being even more problematic during Covid; calls to eliminate the need for peer teaching observations through the end of the 2021–2022 academic year; various ways to slow down the tenure clock; and just generally taking Covid into account for promotion, tenure, merit, and other processes. But above all, at the heart of it all was this concept of "grace," one that seems increasingly relevant beyond Covid.

Were it to be implemented we believe that the Covid Legacy Project indicates a way forward through some of the choppy waters we have been navigating. It is not wizardry. It will not conquer administrative fecklessness, venality, duplicity, cravenness, or malice. But the idea at its heart, of grace for faculty who try to provide it for our students, even if occasionally in the form of tough love, seems like a promising way forward especially for those of us surrounded by those unicorns: administrators acting in good faith.

Texas Messes with Higher Ed

But then Texas decided to go full-Texas.

In the 2023 legislative session (the Texas Legislature meets in odd-numbered years, giving a year for some of the worst ideas in America to marinate before being implemented) higher education was firmly in the cross hairs. As in so many states, the rural tilt of representation, augmented with a healthy dose of gerrymandering, makes a conservative state seem even more conservative than it is. While Democrats have not won a state-wide race since the late, great Ann Richards left the scene, those elections have also not been all that lopsided—the state tends to lean Republican by about a 53 percent to 47 percent margin, give or take. But because the malefactors of politics can manipulate state-level and U.S. House of Representative races, the Republican Party holds a supermajority. However, unlike a lot of states, and contrary to general trends historically in the legislative branch of the United States as a whole, in the Texas legislature, the Senate tends to carry the weight of the craziest, cruelest ideas with the House as the voice of moderation.

In Texas the Lieutenant Governor has enormous power to set the agenda, and Dan Patrick has carried that role with all of the MAGA-fueled culture war zest he can muster with the full backing of Governor Greg Abbott. In 2023 he targeted three areas of higher education that will be familiar to those watching these trends nationwide—the elimination of: Critical Race Theory (CRT) in university classrooms; offices of Diversity, Equity, and Inclusion (DEI) and their affiliated apparatuses; and Tenure.

The CRT legislation went nowhere, in no small part because even in using CRT as a bogeyman legislators had no idea what they were eliminating. Not that ignorance has ever been an impediment when the Texas Legislature wants to throw its weight around, but the anti–CRT proposals failed. The elimination of DEI is another matter—that legislation passed and its deleterious effects are being felt around the state as universities, under pressure from politicians, have been firing people and stripping offices. Whatever DEI's excesses—and there were some, as often happens when offices become entrenched and people think their work is the most important work at an institution—thousands of students now run the risk of being left behind because a bunch of politicians slayed a creature largely conjured in their imagination. The tenure legislation was the most interesting in some ways. What began as an effort to eliminate the granting of tenure to any new faculty in Texas, thus allowing it to wither on the vine within a generation, ended up being a bill that for the first time actually entrenched tenure in state law. But even this seeming victory came with the requirement for universities to draft policies to fire tenured faculty members, a task that not a few university presidents and their various lackeys have tackled with something approaching barely disguised glee. Some of those presidents and many of those lackeys (far too many provosts, far from being Chief Academic Officers are really just Despots in Training, waiting for their own chance to run a university aground) are almost certainly going to go after tenured faculty just as soon as they can. At least some of those cases will have more to do with going after vocal challengers to their power, not after faculty who are unproductive or incompetent.

But there is no rest for the weary. Or the wicked. Dan Patrick has already laid out the broad contours of his agenda for 2025. Rising like a phoenix is the CRT legislation, this time being couched as "divisive concepts" legislation. This will, of course, make teaching history, sociology, political science, and myriad other disciplines where anything is divisive to someone, nearly impossible. Even in an environment where apocalyptic language tends to be common, this really would be a death knell for academic freedom, and, indeed, for academia as we know it. Similarly, the sages in Austin plan to revisit tenure—in theory to see how the implementation of the firing policies is going, but at least a few legislators seem committed to taking another bite at the apple to eliminate tenure. A final, and new, issue is that the legislature is going to look at faculty senates. We do not know what that means, but we suspect that it is not good coming from a bunch of people who firmly believe in top-down autocratic leadership. Given the quality of some of our university presidents and provosts, this is especially alarming for not only shared governance, but again, for academic freedom.

The strangest thing is that most of us just want to be left alone. Or at least we want to be left alone in those areas where we flourish. Left alone to teach our classes and the students we care about. Left alone to engage in our scholarship and writing and creative work. Where we want to collaborate, in our service work, and especially in shared governance, many institutions have made clear that they don't want our input. Or that shared governance is little more than a headache. Beware the upper-level administrator who claims to value dissent and the back-and-forth. They usually don't. They are a subset of the administrator who leads a conversation with "remember, I am a faculty member too!" If they have to say it, they ain't it, and when they do say it, keep an eye on your pay stub, your academic freedom, and your curriculum, because at least one of those things is in trouble. As a corollary to this principle, one of the more vexing elements of modern academia is the haughty way that administrators who have not been in a classroom in decades (if ever) try to claim that they speak for student rights, student interests, and student success in the face of those of us who work with and interact with students every day. When administrators start claiming the mantle of student interests ("Won't somebody please think of the children!") one can be reasonably certain that the students are the human shield as the administration lobbies for things that are probably not actually in the interest of students, at least not in the long run.

My guess is that the battle lines are only going to become more firmly entrenched in the wake of the April and May 2024 protest movements on a number of American campuses. In Texas the most visible of these has been at the University of Texas at Austin, the flagship of my state system. And one certainly has to know that politicians are preparing to take their pound of flesh out of those students but especially those arrogant professors. But in Texas, as in most places, the old Jerry Tarkanian line comes to the fore as one of the great metaphors in American academic life. "Tark the Shark," a longtime basketball coach most famous for leading the University of Nevada–Las Vegas to a national championship, and one of the most voluble, volatile thorns ever to twist in the side of the NCAA, was once heard to say, "The NCAA is so mad at Kentucky that they're going to give Cleveland State another year of probation." In other words, mighty Kentucky is largely untouchable, whatever they did to anger the NCAA, and blueblood Kentucky has myriad ways to protect itself, but little Cleveland State certainly isn't and doesn't. Well, my guess is that the Governor, Lieutenant Governor, and state legislature of Texas are going to be so angry at the University of Texas at Austin that those of us in the hinterlands had better duck.

Conclusion

A few years back, after yet another run-in with administration when I was president of our faculty senate, our provost and I met. That provost had come to my university with a great deal of promise. He came in as a historian who at first legitimately seemed to care about the right things. But he also was ambitious—he wanted to become a university president. I mentioned AAUP policies on academic freedom that he was in the process of violating—and he said, simply, "Who cares about the AAUP?"

I thought that glib rejoinder was telling. After all, the AAUP, a longtime stalwart for academic freedom, has long defended and advocated for the values that helped to make American higher education the envy of the world. It is thus perhaps a particularly bitter irony that the AAUP's authority and status has diminished in similar ways to the diminished authority and status of the faculty at most universities. Yet no other country on Earth has the quantity and quality of colleges and universities that the United States enjoys, even taking into account population size. We allow a vast swath of our population to try out higher education, and institutions like mine turn that opportunity into promise, and that promise into results. All most of us want to do is continue to pursue, create, and disseminate knowledge. It is unfortunate that this generation of politicians and administrators seems bound and determined to destroy this one unalloyed good, something respected far more than our military or our politics. But bound and determined they seem to be.

A Chronicle of Exile

Douglas Higbee

The listed author found the following notes on the desktop hard-drive of a departmental colleague who never returned from a Fulbright year teaching abroad. For privacy reasons this colleague will not be named. These notes have been lightly edited for readability. Names and incidental identifying information have been changed to protect both the innocent and the guilty.

Proto-Professor

1. August 1990. Disorient Express. On summer break from ElitePubU I take a two-month backpacking trip across Eastern Europe, part of an informal group of seven or eight other students and a history professor. We visit several capitals and take a few country excursions, including Prague, Budapest and Lake Balaton, Krakow and the Tatras Mountains, East Berlin, the Ukrainian city of Lviv. For an Orange County boy, this is pretty heady stuff, and I am filled with a deep sense of history and the joy of various social encounters. In Bucharest, I see clusters of Stalinist apartment blocks, cafes empty of food, long lines for beer around midnight. Romanian students tell me of the recent miners' rampage at the University of Bucharest, spurred on by nationalist politicians. They ask me to set up student exchanges and other means of assistance when I return to college. I try to do so but fail.

2. August 1991. Noblesse Oblige. I ask a professor at ElitePubU to sign my override enrollment form for his course on movie Westerns. He gladly obliges, as if he has done so hundreds of times, and I become one of over 300 students in the lecture-based course.

3. November 1991. I am what I Play. I begin DJ-ing at the college radio station. With its several rooms full of LPs, there's few records

I can't find. I play *Exile*-era Rolling Stones, The Clash, Minutemen, Replacements, some new band called Nirvana to anyone who might be listening during my 3–6 a.m. time slot.

    4. May 1993. That Just Happened. The ElitePubU English department holds its graduation in the outdoor Classical Amphitheater. We wait, capped and gowned, for our turn to shake hands with the department chair and receive our diplomas. I'm in line with friends whom I've known since our freshman days in the dorms. Shane and I would run the fire trail up the hills to the Nobel Museum of Science and go to punk rock shows at Bishop Square. Shep would hook us up with good weed and show us how to light our farts on fire. Just ahead of me in line, Shep does a cartwheel across the stage, sticking the landing, hand outstretched for the paper.

    5. October 1993. Fired. For several months since graduation I've been working at a fancy wine shop in downtown EconSegCity, combination barkeep, cashier, and stockboy. Three people co-own the shop, and I am the only employee. Joe, the spitting image of Wally George, pays me every week in cash to avoid payroll taxes. Harold manages the stock, and I don't know what Carmen does. The best part of the job is the samplings of wines I could never afford. Joe regularly introduces me to this or that wine, and customers often share bottles from their newly purchased cases of Montrachet or Romanee Conti. Pretty soon I get used to the mid-afternoon wine buzz. One hot day I'm unloading about 100 cases from a delivery truck parked outside. Boxed in rough pine, each case easily weighs 75 pounds. I'm almost done unloading, and I pause to wipe my brow. Harold comes out to hector me for lagging. "Chop chop," he barks. Why don't you move some fucking cases yourself, I hastily inquire. The next day before work Joe calls me with the news that my services will no longer be needed. Some years later, it turns out, Joe is convicted of embezzlement—as featured on CNBC's *Lazy Fair* show, he used the rather large customer deposits on upcoming Burgundy and Bordeaux releases to finance some rather lavish personal spending—and serves several years behind bars.

    6. January 1994. Fired Again. For several months I've been truck-delivering for a local bagel company. The job provides free food and is largely unsupervised, at least when I'm out on delivery. While waiting around the warehouse for another load of bagels I read the Norton anthologies of British and American Literature in preparation for the GRE. The owner—a nice guy, an entrepreneurial ex-hippie—sees me munching free bagels and reading one time too many times and fires me.

    7. August 1994–June 1997. Substitute. I fill in a couple days a week at various schools in EconSeg School District. ESSD is a social kaleidoscope:

one day I could be up in the hills settling cuddly kindergartners down for a nap, another day I could be attempting to redirect the boredom and frustration of high schoolers in the flatlands. Without a car, I take the city bus; because EconSeg runs many miles north to south, from my rented room in neighboring LibMec it usually takes 45–75 minutes to reach the appropriate destination. One time I sub at a high school at the outset of the Ebonics initiative; a local TV news crew comes into my class to interview students. Another time a student throws an eraser at me while my back is turned; more than once I am challenged to fight.

    8. April 1996. Bon Voyage. I ask my literary theory professor for a letter of recommendation for my Ph.D. applications. Where are you applying, she asks. Among other places I mention UniNewTheory. I don't know much about the program, but it is close to where my girlfriend is herself a Ph.D. student at a neighboring school. Well, she says, no one from our school has ever gotten in there.

    9. August 1997. Lowered Expectations. At my first UniNewTheory grad student party, I wear my best (and only) sportscoat and liberally share cigarettes from my aluminum case. My grad student host serves Busch light, and his biology roommate keeps flatworms in the fridge.

    10. March 1998. Pecking Order. I am asked, politely, by the secretary not to smoke on the second floor balcony outside the English and Comparative Literature department office. Later that day I notice Pre-Eminent French Theorist in the same spot, smoking his pipe.

    11. November 1998. Vulgar Marxist. In Eminent American Theorist's seminar, I present a paper on his favorite author, Thomas Hardy. I choose Hardy's worst poem, "The Men Who March Away," a bit of patriotic crap written at the start of the First World War. Later in office hours, Theorist, ever the gentleman, politely encourages me to look for something more "interesting." I go on a rant on how "interesting" is merely an analytical criterion for formalist subterfuge.

    12. January 2001. I'll Take Adorno for $400, Alex. I use my appearance on a TV game show as an excuse for not submitting my dissertation prospectus on time.

    13. June 2004. I officially earn my Ph.D. My dissertation is typed in courier font. I do not attend graduation ceremonies.

First Impressions

    1. October 2004. Together with a dozen other schools, I apply to the university at which I am now employed. When I am selected for an interview, I have to look up the name of the town on a map.

2. February 2005. Campus Interview. I stay at a charming bed and breakfast. I give a teaching demonstration, meet with the search committee, etc. After lunch the department chair takes me for a town tour. He points to the house of a local 19th-century poet I pretend to have heard of. We pass by Walmart, and then, a few minutes later, another Walmart. I have a nice chat with the chancellor in his office, located in an old antebellum mansion that has been preserved and relocated to campus, and compliment him on his set of golf clubs. At my final meeting of the day, the benefits lady shows me a graph of my projected pension benefit after thirty years.

3. August 2005. Move-in Day. My second-floor office measures approximately 80 square feet and has a narrow vertical window that doesn't open. The federal prison bureau's mandated minimum cell size is 70 square feet.

4. August 2005. Meeting the Boss. Faculty are expected to attend the annual freshman convocation. Provost asks the faculty to line up in the hallway just outside the auditorium. As the new freshman class files out after the convocation proceedings, all blank smiles, we faculty applaud. It will be a few years before I figure out which meetings and activities junior faculty can skip.

5. August 2005. Baptism by Sweat. The department chair has assigned me four sections of freshman composition that meet twice a week. By the time I arrive on campus at 7:30 a.m., with jacket and tie, it is 75 degrees, 90 percent humidity. In the bathroom mirror, I can see the sweat marks blooming on my new Oxford shirt. I appreciate the four-day weekends but I am far from being in 4–4 shape. By the end of the first month, my allegiance to the process-model of writing starts to wither.

6. September 2005. Meeting the Boss, Part II. At my first department meeting, the other faculty enthusiastically discuss several students by name. The department chair discusses enrollment numbers, "assessment," and photocopy limits.

7. November 2005. Love it or Leave it. In grad school, I joined the campus chapter of the UAW, the only union willing to represent graduate student instructors. We had organized grade strikes, to some success. At my present campus, adjunct faculty make $2000 per course. I request a meeting with Provost to discuss the adjunct faculty issue. When Provost was an English professor, she published a book about literary representations of labor (with a university press; you really have to check these days). We have a cordial conversation. Toward the end of our meeting, Provost professes her belief in the "free market system." Later that year Provost awards me a course release for research. The course will be staffed by an adjunct.

8. December 2005. All in the Family. The University starts the "Family Fund" program—all faculty and staff are expected to contribute to the University's annual fundraising campaign. We are told that a high faculty and staff contribution rate—no matter the actual amount—will be interpreted by outside donors that the University is full of dedicated, selfless people who sacrifice (voluntarily) for the betterment of their institution. I think of serfs making a harvest basket for the lord. We are regularly informed via email of the contribution rates of this or that department: Great news! Kinesiology has hit the 100 percent mark! The end of the campaign is punctuated by a special celebration with speeches and door prizes.

9. February 2006. A longtime member of the department—who bears more than a passing resemblance to a sad Santa Claus—lists an unsuccessful grant application in his faculty bio. I ask him out for a beer, and he declines. Many of the long-time faculty look burned out and beat up.

10. April 2006. Housewarming. The first evening in our new house, a large thunderstorm darkens the sky. The next day I hear on the local news that a tornado destroyed several trailers a few miles away. Later this month, I use a lawnmower for the first time in my life.

11. May 15–August 15, 2006. Summer Break. The humidity keeps me inside and thus my summers productive. I send out three articles, prepare two new courses, and frequently check the Chronicle's job listings. Thus begins my workaholism.

12. October 2006. Faculty Only. My favorite part of our office building is the faculty-only bathroom. It's nice to take care of one's business without a student—perhaps one from one's own class—observing the process. And it's nice to have at least one clear-cut faculty privilege. I assume non-teaching, upper-level administrators—not being faculty presently—are not allowed to use this bathroom, and the fantasy of catching them *en flagrante delicto* is a delicious one, notwithstanding the context. Though there is a slight downside to the faculty bathroom. It is accessible only from within the regular bathroom, and is designed to accommodate only one person at a time. Thus, when on occasion one's entry into the faculty bathroom is denied by its being occupied, one is obliged to endure a walk of shame to the student stalls or urinals.

13. January 2007. The iPhone 1 is released. I keep my flip phone.

14. January 2007. Collaborative Teaching. My next-door office neighbor, who tends to wear her feminism on her sleeve, informs me that the history professor with whom I am team-teaching a new course is a sexual "predator," and that association with him might, at such a

tender stage in my career, tarnish my collegial profile in the eyes of my colleagues, some of whom may even be on the promotion and tenure committee. She offers no evidence for such crimes beyond hearsay. I continue team-teaching the class.

15. February 2007. My faculty mentor, just retired, dies suddenly.

16. May 2007. Extra Curriculars. A friend in the department, a former Army Ranger, bails me out of jail for DUI. I proceed to have the best tasting cigarette of my life. A first-time offender, I am given the option of an intervention program, with counseling and community service, if I plead *nolo contendere*. For the next several months, I complete court-mandated tasks such as attend AA meetings and community service at a local Disabled American Veterans center. The highlight of the intervention program is the scared straight day at a nearby prison. I am part of a group of about 20 other offenders, most of them kids who got caught with marijuana or Xanax. We are quick-stepped through the yard, regaled with cautionary tales from long-time prisoners, visit a cell or two, and heartily encouraged to sample the cafeteria staple referred to as "prison loaf."

Third-Sixth Year

1. October 2008. The Natives. My Obama campaign sign has gone missing from the front lawn, for the second time. I suspect my next-door neighbor, a friendly man with a surly wife who owns a six-wheeled diesel pickup truck, a riding mower for a lawn half the size of mine, an RV, a golf cart, and a large boat, but I don't investigate. His elementary school daughter once told me she wants to be a physical therapist.

2. September 2009. Best in Show. My university is awarded Best Regional Comprehensive University by U.S. News for the fourth year in a row.

3. November 2009. Don't Stand So Close. I am teaching a course on the work of D.H. Lawrence. One of the students, a young, divorced mother, often stays after class to chat, often visits my office hours, and sends me frequent emails, especially after we finish *Lady Chatterley's Lover*. She is a very good writer, one has to admit.

4. December 2009. My first book is published, an edited essay collection. In the months ahead I relish reading the reviews and feeling like a real scholar.

5. May 2011. I receive official notification from the Board of Trustees that I have been promoted to associate professor, with tenure.

I affix the letter to my bulletin board with a thumbtack, and place my tenure application binder on the bookshelf.

Homo Academicus

   a. *Homo academicus* is real.
   b. *Homo academicus* is a faculty member at every non–R1 college and university in the United States.
   c. *Homo academicus* has a name, and it is Chris.
   d. Chris is an advanced assistant or newly tenured associate professor in the humanities and social sciences.
   e. Chris is a very nice person.
   f. Chris never utters a statement without at least three qualifying phrases.
   g. Chris sits on every administration-appointed committee and is everyone's choice for chair.
   h. Chris dresses neatly and wears low-prescription glasses.
   i. Chris has apologized over 1,000 times since beginning graduate school.
   j. Chris is a model employee and is well-liked by the campus administration.
   k. Chris is aware of the systemic oppression Chris' ancestors practiced and which Chris' present existence perpetuates.
   l. Chris accepts without complaint the administration's raising of enrollment caps, insurance premiums, and funds for the new Musk School of Artificial Intelligence.
   m. Chris never asks an inconvenient question during faculty assembly meetings.
   n. Chris is ruthless on the pickleball court.
   o. Chris is sympathetic to your mental health issues.
   p. Chris always understands your perspective.
   q. Chris accepts the downsizing of his department with equanimity.

Post-Tenure

   1. 2005–2013. A Community in Exile. Most of my department colleagues with whom I am friendly are also new to the area, with young families too. We quickly become a close group, and frequently congregate at each other's homes for dinner parties, kid's birthdays, etc.

We drink beer and talk shop while our significant others drink wine and complain about their significant others. We play music together on our back porches, and go on trips to the coast together. That all comes to a halt when one of us becomes department chair.

    2. March 2014. Rape Culture. At a department meeting, I use the word "rape" in reference to the campus administration's attitude toward the liberal arts and "shared governance." No one at the meeting objects to my argument or my wording. A week later, the department chair summons me to his office to inform me that another faculty member in our department—unspecified, of course—has complained about my use of the word. One would think that of all people English faculty would be well-attuned to the difference between literal and figurative language, as well as context.

    3. September 2015. Sticker Shock. I find out that the business faculty at my university make approximately double what we faculty in the humanities make. "Market forces," says Provost.

    4. November 2017. Rubber Stamp. This is my second year on the promotion and tenure committee, which vets and ranks candidates for final approval by Provost, the Chancellor, and eventually the Board of Trustees. The committee is comprised of faculty from various units throughout the university. After candidates submit their copious files, committee members read through them (or skim, more accurately) and prepare notes for the big meeting, at which we discuss each file and vote whether to recommend a candidate for promotion and/or tenure. I pay most attention to the scholarship listed on the CV and skim the external reviews. On more than one occasion a candidate lists articles from pseudo-journals with names like *The International Journal of Research*. One year, a candidate includes a blog entry about cooking. My naysaying never prevails.

    5. March 2018. My fourth book is published. I don't need to do that amount of scholarship to be promoted. I do it because I am bored and in the slight chance of getting a different job.

    6. October 2018. A Shout Out to Shared Governance. New Provost announces via email that the English department will be amalgamated with the Department of Foreign Languages. Faculty have not been notified or consulted. At the next Faculty Assembly meeting, I question Provost on his decision. How could you treat faculty this way, I ask, people whose dedication to their profession is largely based on a strong sense of semi-autonomy? What sort of leadership is this? Provost is a friendly, often humorous man. He looks at me for a moment, then glances rather anxiously over at the Chancellor, seated in the front row. She keeps her poker face.

7. October 2018. Why Academe Can Suck. I'm on a roundtable at the big annual conference for literature types. We are given strict instructions by the chair (a friend and research collaborator) not to go over the 10-minute time limit. I do my 10 minutes. The 'star' of the panel blows through his time limit without comment from the chair, and during the Q&A enthusiastically welcomes an audience member's recitation of a literature-themed rap. I stifle, and ruminate on the entrepreneurial nature of scholarship.

8. June 2019. F**k You, Money. I receive final confirmation from the Board of Trustees that I have been promoted to full professor. There is a decent raise included. Two days later, I receive a *pro forma* email from Provost informing me that my endowed chair has not been renewed. No reason is given.

9. March 2020. Impermanent Vacation. The Covid pandemic closes the campus, and we transition to online teaching. I have never even used Blackboard before. With the gracious help of our technology director, that transition is made fairly easily. I don't teach another in-person class for nearly a year. Frankly, this interruption provides a much-needed break from the grind of the classroom. My dogs soon become spoiled with the extra attention.

10. March 2021. The Needle and the Damage Done. The University has returned to in-person instruction. The department chair informs me that a student has informed their advisor, who informed their dean, who then informed Provost, that I offer extra credit to students who can provide proof of Covid vaccination. Provost is not happy, he says. Guilty as charged, I say. The chair informs me that such extra credit violates university policy. I ask what policy he is referring to. He refers to an email sent to the faculty over the summer by Provost. That isn't exactly a policy, I reply, that's one line in an email that I didn't read because I'm not on contract in the summer. The chair tells me either I rescind the extra credit policy or face "severe disciplinary action."

11. June 2021. Victoria, just retired, dies of cancer. Victoria taught at my university for decades and ran the writing center.

12. "Preach the word; be prepared in season and out of season; correct, rebuke and encourage—with great patience and careful instruction. For the time will come when people will not put up with sound doctrine. Instead, to suit their own desires, they will gather around them a great number of teachers to say what their itching ears want to hear. They will turn their ears away from the truth and turn aside to myths. But you, keep your head in all situations, endure hardship, do the work of an evangelist, discharge all the duties of your ministry. For I am already being poured out like a drink offering, and

the time for my departure is near. I have fought the good fight, I have finished the race, I have kept the faith" (2 Timothy 4).

13. September 2022. The Heart of the Matter. The cardiologist attaches a heart monitor to my partially shaven chest. The heart monitor looks like a thick, six-inch bandage, with a computer chip that sends signals to the phone that I am told to keep with me for the next month. The cardiologist tells me he is 81 years old and gets up every day at 4 a.m. My father died suddenly at age 45.

14. October 2022. Escape Plan. I apply for a year-length Fulbright grant to teach in Eastern Europe.

15. November 2022. Who's Afraid of Virginia Woolf. The department chair tells me another professor in our department has filed a Title VII complaint against me. I look up what Title VII is. Apparently, my silly pun over the last name of a Native American visiting writer did not sit well. This pun was not broadcast but offered to another colleague during a casual chat inside their office. When asked about the incident by HR, this same colleague described the incident as a harmless joke, and the complaint has been summarily dismissed. The department chair tells me he is extra careful these days about what he says. "People are so touchy."

16. November 2022. A Terrible New Genre is Born. Before my morning classes, for kicks, I file a Title IX complaint against the person I suspect filed the Title VII complaint against me earlier in the week. I load the complaint with histrionic language that, I hope, renders it as close to satire as possible. My intention is to combine a "fuck you" to my complaining adversary with a "fuck off" to the HR people who take this stuff seriously:

Please provide a detailed description of the incident/concern using specific, concise, and objective language (who, what, where, when, why, and how).

The alleged has publicly posted a printed photo on the alleged's office door in which a young man is ogling a young woman from behind while his girlfriend looks on in dismay (I understand this image is also an online "meme" titled "Disloyal Man"). In the photo, the young man is captioned "Dr. Amwitch"—referring, of course, to the alleged. The young woman being ogled is captioned "well-written essays." The offended girlfriend is captioned "Dr. Amwitch's students."

This photo is offensive because it reduces the young woman to a sexual object, one whose primary value is located in her hind parts, and objectifies the young man as a sexual harasser, unable to control his field of vision. In addition, the alleged has assumed the subject position of a sexual harasser, which is rather offensive as well. Lastly, the photo suggests that the writer-reader relationship is inherently heterosexual, which I find to be quite discriminatory against non-heterosexuals. If the university can no longer be a safe space for English departments, it should at least be one for student essays.

The next day, HR replies to me that the offending photo has been taken down. I check, and indeed it has been.

17. December 2022. Corner Office. A friendly colleague is retiring this year. Admin has declined hiring a replacement for his position. The English department takes another hit. I ask the department chair who will get the soon-to-be-empty corner office. It's about twice the size of mine. I mention I'm next in line in terms of seniority. The chair says he wants it. "But I've been here longer than you," I say. "Why the change in tradition?" "Because I can," he says. I may have muttered, "Fuck yourself" as I exit the chair's office.

18. January 2023. Zoo Story. At a department meeting, we discuss next fall's class schedule—who will teach which classes, etc. This is more than a fill-in-the-blanks exercise, as our dwindling population of majors has impacted our teaching assignments. Ever since I was hired over 15 years ago, the teaching load for tenure-track faculty is two composition courses and two literature courses. That can vary. Someone might get a course release on a research grant. Sometimes, an upper-level literature course is cancelled from lack of enrollment. Etc.

The chair is making a list on the board—we meet in a classroom—of who plans to teach what. We all chime in. Our early Americanist, Eliza, says she's only teaching two courses in the fall—she has a new administrative role outside the department—and asks for two sections of an American lit survey.

The discussion is about to wind up, but I raise my hand. "Eliza," I ask, addressing her directly, "wouldn't it be fairer if you taught one composition course and just one section of the literature survey? After all, we normally divide our literature and composition teaching in half, and plus there'd then be more students to fill our other literature courses." Her eyes widen above her coronavirus mask. "I don't appreciate you putting me on the spot like this," she says, scanning the room for allies, and proceeds to excuse her course choices because of her heavy service load, the supposed requirement that 1 of her sections be online, etc. The rest of the conversation is muddy in my memory. I do recall using the phrase "get over it," prompting a wounded "hey!" from Eliza. She quickly leaves the room as soon as the meeting adjourns. I let the weekend go by, then send a polite email to Eliza explaining that my comments at Friday's meeting were not personal. No reply.

19. February 2023. It's not me, it's you. The department chair emails me a letter of reprimand, cc'ing the Dean, Provost, and HR. Among my offenses are challenging Eliza at the most recent department meeting, and my telling him (allegedly) to "fuck himself,"

my coronavirus vaccine extra credit, etc. The chair is the same person who bailed me out of jail a decade ago. In my response letter, I don't exactly retract the "fuck yourself" and try to explain that while the chair does usually make the trains run on time, faculty are not trains.

20. March 2023. I receive notice that my Fulbright grant application has been successful, and I'll be teaching in Hungary next year.

> *At this point the notes end. Seated outside a café in Budapest while attending a conference, a friend reports seeing our vanished colleague walk by. Department chair reports that Provost recently received an anonymous email with a link to a cryptic YouTube video from Ukraine, but cannot confirm it was sent by our colleague. After a few months of emails and other queries, our department requests a replacement search. Provost elects not to hire a replacement and transfers the faculty slot to engineering.*

At Your Service
Faculty Workload and Self-Advocacy

Erin B. Jensen

This is the holiday card that I sent to family and friends one recent December:

> I am glad to have the opportunity to live my dream of being an English professor and appreciate the feeling of being needed and wanted by the college. Sometimes, a little too needed though. This semester I am teaching 7 different classes, am the Director of the Writing Center, created a Research Conference for students, direct the school newspaper, coordinate English internships, provide leadership for all Writing classes, created new minors, and participate in eight different committees. Somewhere in my free time, I also publish articles and present at conferences. Whew! My goal for the new year is to start saying "No" to projects.

My card sums up the reality of working at both a small state college and a small private liberal arts college, and I have found the experience to be similar between them. There are many opportunities to be involved in a wide variety of projects, but rarely is there funding or compensation for such efforts. There are many requests for supporting academic programs and too few "collegial" ways to say no.

In my Ph.D. program at a large research university I taught five classes a year, usually two classes in the Fall and three classes in the Spring. I knew that teaching at a small state college would mean an increase in my class load and thought I could handle the increase as I was formerly a high school English teacher. I went through various training classes on how to teach freshman composition and pedagogy related to teaching as part of my Ph.D. program. But I found that most of the conversations about life after the Ph.D. focused mostly on research expectations and publishing. While a tenure-track position at a research focused university would be focused more on research and publications, the reality at many small state universities and colleges is a focus on teaching and very little support or encouragement to publish. While I enjoyed my Ph.D. experience, I did find that the experience did not prepare me for the reality of a tenure-track job at a small state college.

When I was on the job market, I found that many state colleges and universities required a 4/4 load or even a 5/5 load. My first job came with a 5/5 teaching load. This was at an institution that had been a community college and then had added several bachelor's degrees, but still kept the 5/5 teaching requirement. I knew that I was going to be teaching a lot more than I had done during my Ph.D., but I thought I could handle the five classes each semester. I was very surprised to discover that the expectation in the department was that everyone taught overloads and the only semester I actually taught five classes was my very first semester. All other semesters included several overloads, and I usually averaged at least eight classes the two years I taught there. At my current position, as I mentioned in my holiday card, I taught seven different classes (all three-credit classes or 21 credits total) in a mixture of both online and in-person classes. I taught more credits than most college students took! At both colleges, this was a usual occurrence as there was a need for classes to be taught and yet the college didn't want to hire more people to teach the classes. Some semesters were "easier" as I still taught seven classes, but I had several sections of the same class and so could re-use activities from class to class. Semesters where I had to teach seven different classes were semesters where I felt exhausted in trying to come up with new activities for each class.

I had one family member email me after she had received my holiday card and ask me how it was possible to be so busy. She also jokingly wrote, "well, at least you are getting paid to be involved in so many things and so that must help you out financially!" Unfortunately, she is largely mistaken. At my current college, I am paid for the four classes in my contract and then paid at an adjunct rate (which is significantly less) for any classes beyond those four. I am also not paid for the three-credit hour class for the students involved in internships, even though students have assignments and I have to meet with them about their progress. When I asked why I wasn't paid for this class, I was told that they had never paid for the internship class and if I wasn't willing to teach it, then students wouldn't be able to get college credit for internships. I am a passionate advocate and supporter of students having internships and so I agreed not to be paid so that the class can be offered. I am also not paid for directing the school newspaper, even though I usually spend between 100 and 200 hours of my own time each semester editing and formatting the newspaper. Again, when I asked why I wasn't paid, I was told that the college has never paid for any faculty to direct the newspaper, but if I quit then the college would no longer have a newspaper. So, I continued to direct the newspaper until this past semester for free.

Another large impact on my free time is directing the Writing Center. That role involves either getting a course release or salary for one course at adjunct rates, but not both. I usually take the money, but it depends on the semester. I am not paid for any leadership I provide to the college or the training of adjuncts that I also participate in. None of my Ph.D. discussions about tenure-track jobs ever discussed the lack of funding in small colleges or that this is a common problem. The lack of getting paid for my efforts is a common theme in all of my state college experience.

I read a rough draft of this chapter to some friends and the main feedback I received was why would I stay in a job like this. I do want to assert that I love teaching and having the opportunity to work with students. I stay because of the students and because of seeing the improvement and progress students make over four years. I stay because I enjoy having an opportunity to have a student as a freshman and then have them in several other classes and maybe even have an opportunity to help them apply to graduate school. Small colleges provide opportunities for students to get to know their professors in ways that large universities do not. I stay for the students and for my contributions to their academic success.

Administrators and college staff know how passionate I am about helping students and use this information to their benefit. Many people know that if you want me to be involved in any project, you simply have to tell me that it will benefit the academic success of students, and I will get involved in the project. This is a weakness of mine that is often exploited for the good of the college and students, but severely reduces my free time and makes a work-life balance extremely difficult.

At all the small state colleges I have worked, there has always been a lot of need for student support, not enough money to provide that support, and too many opportunities to say "yes." Also, no one in administration has advocated for me to teach fewer classes or be involved less. I have found that the only person that advocates for me is myself, and I do not do a good job at that. I continue to need to work on creating better boundaries for myself and my time.

Whenever I mention this teaching load to other professors around the country, many are horrified. A few years ago, my department was audited by a professor from a different state college on the other side of the state. She interviewed all the professors individually and asked us about what our responsibilities were and what projects we were involved in. At the end of my interview, she expressed admiration for all that I was doing, but did tell me she was very concerned about my ability to maintain such a schedule, and she encouraged me not to continue doing so. She reiterated to me that I needed to advocate for my own mental and physical well-being and that if I didn't, she didn't think anyone else would either. She shared the example of when you get on an airplane with a child, the flight attendants will always remind the parent to put on their oxygen mask first before putting the mask on the child. She related this to my situation of putting masks on everyone else and that I can't hold my breath forever.

I should mention that I have plenty of colleagues who show up and teach their four classes each semester and then go home. They don't feel any need to teach more than the allotted four or to get involved in lots of different projects. I don't judge those colleagues. Personally, I appreciate the opportunity to create new classes and programs and contribute to other programs. I just find that I not only let myself get too involved but that the college is only too happy to let me do so. Advocacy for self is something that I am trying to learn, but that doesn't come easily for someone with a people-pleasing personality.

In addition to the number of classes, the required service work, and committee work, there is still an expectation to publish and present at conferences. My state college job provided no travel funding for conferences and did not encourage publications. I ended up writing a lot of travel grants and mainly attending local conferences I could drive to. I did publish a few articles but quickly realized that no one in my department cared and so I did not mention them. At my current liberal arts college position, I do have a small travel stipend and so still mainly attend local or online conferences. I find that publication is necessary for tenure, but the requirement for publication is very low and while I do let colleagues know when I publish, most people are not interested or supportive. The main emphasis in the tenure process is on teaching evaluations and service to the college.

If my Ph.D. student self could see where I am now and what I am involved in, I think she would be quite surprised, and not in a good way. She would be happy that I love teaching and working with students. But she would be shocked to see me teaching so many different classes and being involved in so many committees without financial compensation. She would have thought the opportunities to teach overloads would be few and occur mainly in the summer. Her teaching would be valued to the point of only teaching the required number of classes. Perhaps one committee would be enough to contribute to the college and her occasional attendance at a faculty meeting would be plenty. She would be concerned at the toll so many classes and committees have on her time and mental health, and she would wonder why she had accepted this job in the first place. My Ph.D. self would probably recognize, though, that my basic personality is to help, or try to help, and would probably recommend that I try to teach less.

As I stated in my holiday card, I do need to do a better job of saying "No" to projects, especially because I need to advocate for myself and my time, and recognize that most small colleges have many needs and that I cannot address them all by myself.

From Professor to Comedian and Back Again

A Case Study of Infusing Academics with Comedy

MATTHEW MCKEAGUE

In this essay, I will discuss an early career challenge as the first new professor in a department for decades, the pushback received when I left to pursue a comedy career in Los Angeles, and how conventional wisdom proved to be wrong when I easily returned to teaching years later with a killer CV in a much better place. No, I won't badmouth previous employers or burn any bridges, as I pester my students to *not* do that daily and I don't want to be a complete hypocrite. But I do plan to address the power of well-timed departures to become a more effective teacher and researcher, all while avoiding the post-tenure depression that's pretty well documented in our increasingly strange career.

Knowing when to leave an academic job is much like being in a toxic relationship, sinking ship, or—worse yet—a toxic relationship *on* a sinking ship. (There had to be at least one combative couple on the *Titanic*, right?) I hope that my valuable learning experience will benefit up-and-coming academics who may stay somewhere in fear of the unknown, tugged back in the ol' crab bucket before realizing their non-crabcake potential. The funniest part of my early career challenge is that I'm not bitter at all, but more on that later. My field, media, is ultimately about storytelling so I've done my best to captivate you in a three-act structure. That's correct, I've housed this insight into an occasionally humorous tale that should inspire people without getting me fired in the process.

So begins the First Act of my story, graduating with a doctorate at the barely ripe age of 27 and then landing an Assistant Professor job at a far older state university near Philadelphia. And there I was, enticed by the prospect of helping students in an exciting way, as well as being able to afford a diet way healthier than Pop-Tarts by the stack. And I can't forget the healthcare benefits which, after the grad school diet I just mentioned, were very much needed. It's here where my first major mental battle occurred on the job—agreeing to do as much as possible to please others. This sometimes-unspoken aspect of a junior faculty member's first years is not unique, as the "fresh meat" feels obligated to say "sure" on repeat. Thus, we wind up teaching way out of our wheelhouse while sitting on every department sub-sub-sub-committee in existence.

The junior faculty must, of course, express agreement to such requests with multiple exclamation points to ensure there's no perceived fatigue or negativity whatsoever. Yes, as the new blood in Full Professor–filled waters, I had been tasked with teaching everything that sunk to the academic floor because no one else wanted to. Table Scraps 101 would be an understatement. Want to teach all our Intro courses *and* oversee the entire Graduate Program? Sure! Want to do that on extreme overload because you're hilariously cheaper? You bet! How about giving TV studio tours to local girl scout troops on the weekends? Absolutely—I don't need to sleep, and I do enjoy their cookies. While some programs protect junior faculty from not being so abruptly obliterated by the request woodchipper, my fate was not so fortunate. And, by the way, I wish I were joking about the girl scout tours.

One instance burned into my brain took place during a department meeting, the type where everyone averts their eyes like a guilty dog when the Chair needs to delegate service duties. Wanting to be a team player for the first request, I volunteered to cover the earliest Open House event, and another faculty member said she would help that day. When getting to the second and third Open Houses, as the others still stared into the vast emptiness of the table or their groins, the Chair looked back at me. "Matt, are you available these dates too?" I didn't have any good excuses compared to theirs, like kids visiting that weekend or hip-replacement surgeries booked months in advance, so call me Mr. Recruitment, I guess! Again, providing some support, at least the same colleague volunteered to help me while the rest did their best impression of a mime.

Yet, what was I to do? Junior faculty know that our colleagues will be evaluating us the next few years and potentially voting to kick us off the academic island, reality TV–style. Refusing anything so early would be just as dumb as telling "Yo Mamma" jokes to your hostage-taker. I respected, and still do, some of these colleagues, but they were truly untouchable compared to my powerless noob status. Yes, I understand that those senior faculty were likely burned out from being overburdened too, but that doesn't mean it's kosher to give all of the grunt work to the person making literally half their salary. I understand why the Chair has to delegate too, of course, as they've had a torrent of dictates from above dumped on them that they can't deal with solo. But the difference is that junior faculty barely scrape by with the litany of peer evaluations, trainings, and enough new class preps that'd put any juggler to shame. If it's something that we'd be angry at our students doing in group work situations, then we should probably stop ourselves too, right? But back then, I had no idea if this was normal or not.

I barely had a personal life and, during the toughest weeks, fought urges to devour an entire box of Pop-Tarts like the old days. Despite those challenges, I quickly became a student favorite even though I wasn't tossing around easy A's or candy on evaluation days. And a few years of polite pushing to protect all faculty's mental health with more equal work distribution, I was in line to be Chair with a cushiony job and an equally comfortable butt imprint. While my academic career was going great in every way, I grew increasingly disheartened with another common development—I had been so busy working up the academic ladder that I completely forgot the very passion that drove me to study media in the first place.

Thus, much to the dismay of those who had not protected me from time-consuming requests, I left for Los Angeles to try out a childhood dream of working in the comedy business. I didn't think I'd become some superstar, but I did believe that I could treat it like an early career sabbatical that no committee would ever grant ... without bribes. Though many of my peers and advisors were supportive of this adventure, some purists warned that such a decision could leave me in the dustbins of perpetual adjunct work, teaching 14,000 classes at half the salary until the robots took over. "And you're risking all that for comedy, Matt? Like, seriously?" Yes, breaking this news to a few of my doctoral professors caused a heck of a lot of "spit-takes" for sure.

So I headed to Los Angeles with no potential job lined up in this tale's Second Act, venturing on a creative pilgrimage that a few of my previous students took. Of course, in the back of my mind, I had worried about becoming yet another waiter with a Ph.D. or carwash attendant skilled at Likert scales, but I figured my background in media and a lifelong comedy passion would get me somewhere. And in less than a month, I landed a job as an article editor and comedy writer for one of the Top 10 mobile traffic websites in the world. I had used the very tactics I taught my students, such as researching the company like an obsessed stalker. Plus, I pitched that I'm the future-proof candidate because I had video production experience should they want to expand into any non-text-based entertainment. It was nice to see that my own tips worked, ultimately.

Literally three days later, I was back at that office now as an employee, taking on every task from crafting Listicles about obscure '80s toys to editing grammar mistakes like the old times—no red pen required this time. Within a few months of writing comedy articles and making my staff's work even funnier, the site took me up on my offer and began producing video comedy sketches with me as a key player. From holding the boom mic for 10 hours in a bar sketch to editing Hello Kitty Convention footage for comedic impact, I got to use every skill I had been honing before that tsunami of academic service took over my past life and drowned my creative output. Though, admittedly, the patience I had learned from committee work, administrative meetings, and parents demanding to know their kids' grades (despite FERPA being a thing) kept me composed no matter the job in California.

The number of new experiences that I would have skipped if I stayed in that soon-to-be Department Chair role still astounds me. Here's a sillier example: I was among the oldest workers on this cool company's creative staff, a complete opposite from my first days in academia. Yes, it was the type of young company led by meme gurus, the folks who didn't let any bureaucracy get in the way. To put it in tangible terms, we had free snacks, basketball hoops, and even video game systems to encourage playful teamwork at the office. Unsurprisingly, those "irresponsible" touches worked! Also in this role, I used my power to protect new writers, provide feedback on every article, and give them as much creative freedom to grow as I could. Though that previous line sounds like some cheesy Hollywood "bookend" moment, just wait, because there's an even more sentimental one coming later. Our company rapidly expanded, doubling our staff in less than a year as we branched out into other areas like comedic documentaries and podcasts. Though the workhours far exceeded my previous three-day-a-week teaching schedule, I found relief knowing two things: (1) that my efforts were going to help brighten someone's day and (2) that nobody would bring a meeting to a fiery full stop because I didn't use Robert's Rules of Order with surgical precision.

After succeeding for roughly two years in the professional comedy biz, I had learned more about new media, diverse staff, and comedy than I could from any book. Yet as with all good stories, my adventure encountered new hurdles when my parents' health both took a turn for the worse. As a single child, I knew that it was my turn to help them stay alive as long as possible like they did for me decades prior. Thus, I left my comedy career on good terms, those youngsters all telling me that I'd have a job waiting when I came back. And while I suspected that one day I would return, my voyage's Third Act would lead me to one last breakthrough—the type revealed via close up and backed by an epic soundtrack. Could I really combine my passions for teaching and comedy like a delicious peer-reviewed sandwich? I had to try.

As I assisted mom and dad, I knew that I'd need some stability during our impending role reversal. And thus, I punched up the CV with all of my exciting Los Angeles experiences and applied to nearby universities to teach yet again. Within a few months, I hit the ground running with another full-time tenure-track position—easily—without any of that so-called blacklisting I was warned of years prior. Yes, I had returned to academia with cutting-edge skills and plenty of wisdom to share with my media students, soon receiving the highest evaluations of my career and making an undeniable difference. But this time, rather than taking on every request possible, I chose the options that aligned with my strengths and comedy background. And both melded into academia quite well despite its sometimes-stuffy and mold spore–filled air.

Back at my next department meeting after the California dreaming, I had to re-start as junior faculty again—this time entering a group wherein only two of the seven professors had tenure. Thus, when I chimed in first this time, I made sure to spin my volunteerism wisely, packed with humor: "It sounds like we have a lot to do. How about we try to split these equally so we all stay sane? Let's make a chart so none of us look like slackers!" Yes, I said that; however, it was delivered with a sly smirk. Fully empowered by the quick pace of Los Angeles and my leveled-up comedic chops, I now felt comfortable using honesty and sardonic humor to make my points. It's amazing how many truth bombs I was able to unleash there, not met with pushback. Laughter became a tremendous bonding tool that broke any uncomfortable ice like an academic jester.

The new workplace was much more democratic too, even the untouchable Associate and Full Professors assisted us with bottom-of-the-barrel tasks. Much like the crowds when I did stand-up comedy, this department had a completely different atmosphere from the first. A cynical take would be that there were simply more junior faculty trying to please people, so the misery was spread out, but that wasn't the only factor. This Chair embraced change and new perspectives, making sure that nobody got bogged down in the tenure-track tarpits. Thus, I felt energized with a new joke-filled approach and a crew of colleagues completing their fair share.

But that was just the start of the new me. For optimal effectiveness, I recommend reading this next paragraph like a training montage of my return to a state university. First up was to form a sketch comedy production student club where I advised funny storytellers. Second, I designed a Comedy Writing and Production course, an experience unique in my state system that attracted students to a field perceived as mysterious. Third, I merged my background and research, becoming a journal-publishing madman with article topics that I never would have dared to in the past: "Weird Al" Yankovic, Mel Brooks, and The Three Stooges to name a few.

And finally, I continued my own creative comedic outlet by publishing three funny books on the side such as a Dr. Seuss parody for adults (*Darker Truths*), an epic-sized nerdy novel (*Andy Gets Conned*), and a purposely stupid comic book (*Dolphin Cop*). Yes, I had figured out how to live both dreams at once—helping students achieve their comedic media goals while working on my own. And, this time, I didn't have to drive two hours in bumper-to-bumper traffic with smog-filled lungs to do it. (All of those books are available on Amazon if you're intrigued, by the way. Hey, I'm never above some shameless self-promotion.)

Now in my second decade of teaching in the same state system at another campus, I still look back at these early career challenges fondly—no Pop-Tarts in sight. If I had stayed at my cushiony professor job the first time, I wouldn't possess the same skillset or insight how to be a teacher and storyteller at once. Plus, students who have taken my classes have gone on to excel in comedic production environments, working at locations such as Comedy Central and Saturday Night Live. I've also been able to continue publishing, such as developing the world's first conceptual framework for The Comic Triple technique of humor, also referred to as The Rule of Three. Thus, the early hurdles I traversed have created an even more enjoyable story arc than I could have imagined. Though similar toxic hiccups may leave one's mouth bitter, I am thankful for the challenges experienced along the way because, without them, I may not have found these far greener (and funnier) pastures in the long run.

For any junior faculty feeling stuck in similar ways, please remember that safe stability can still lead to a life of unfulfilled sub-sub-sub-committees and Robert's Rules of Order sticklers. Of course, you'll always have some of that in any academic position. But if you think you need to make a change, don't let others convince you that it's just some angst-filled misstep or mid-life crisis. Push forward and you'll likely have a better story to tell someday too. If we only get one chance to tell our tale, you don't want your last page to be some stupidly clichéd lamentation about the journey you didn't take. I kinda hate myself for that last line, but hey, I wrote it with a sly smirk.

The Whole Truth, Nothing But
Learning to Teach at a Small Rural University

Louis Young

I. Graduating Brooks

Some years ago, a student thanked me in my office for being one reason he had not quit college. Only half in jest, I replied, "But Brooks, I've failed you four times!" He laughed heartily. This student was among the most knowledgeable I had met. But he had a penchant for leaving things unfinished, starting strong and then disappearing from class. "Self-sabotage" is too harsh—it was a negative cycle of falling slightly behind, becoming discouraged, falling more behind, then losing hope. Over and over again. It certainly wasn't apathy. That semester Brooks regularly attended my Political Philosophy class with a friend and gave a presentation on Sophocles' *Antigone*. Neither of them was enrolled. He was a keystone member of the Southeastern Sideways State University (SSSU) Chess Club, which I sponsored, dutifully attending various on and off-campus community functions. He was also an avid history buff—I learned all about the Boxer and Taiping rebellions, and the making of *Blazing Saddles*, during our chess games. Notwithstanding over a decade of sustained enrollment, his graduation was perennially delayed by a seemingly endless stream of F's and withdrawals, including in courses where he regularly corrected *my* historical mistakes.

When Brooks was two classes from finishing, our department hatched and executed a plan. Step One: When Brooks didn't enroll, we enrolled him without asking and demanded his presence. Step Two: I periodically checked on Brooks' progress with his professors, both in my department, and at our Chess Club. Step Three: When Brooks stopped attending classes around week twelve, we didn't care. It was common knowledge that Brooks would attend Chess Club even when he missed class; and so, over the final month or so, his professors gave me assignments to deliver to Chess Club, and it was my job to follow up. Meanwhile, his academic advisor, with graduation paperwork several months past due, and being unable to get Brooks' signature, gave me that assignment too. At this point Chess Club became more or less a substitute for classes, and I became a third-party negotiator informing Brooks that he was going to graduate, come hell or high water, whether as a reward or punishment, and that, if he didn't graduate this semester, then next semester we would nominate him as our department's Outstanding History Student and seal the deal.

In the end that wasn't necessary. Brooks did graduate. And I still see him every week. He remains a vital member of the Chess Club, attending its weekly meetings and helping run our scholastic chess tournament. He hasn't gotten his diploma, and unless SSSU waives a $30 parking fine I doubt he ever will. The B.A. in History is there for when he needs it, but now is not the time. I expect him at some point to get busy living and move to Jacksonville with friends, and I'll miss him when he goes. But I'll be proud. I'm already proud. He's a treasured member of our community and department. He might be tenured here, for all I know.

Brooks' story hints at the ironies of teaching at SSSU. Helping him graduate required steps I had never dreamt would be part of my job, and that probably shouldn't be part of my job. And while many students at SSSU graduate handily—a large number are academically spectacular, even brilliant—that is not the archetype of our institution. For many others, perhaps a majority of our students, the road to graduation is no less complicated and circuitous than Brooks', and helping these students overcome life's challenges and graduate is the core of my job. It is not easy—when I recently completed a 7.5-hour training in Mental Health First Aid, I spent as much time reflecting on my own mental health symptoms as those of my students. My self-assessment included depression, anxiety, sleeplessness, suicidal thoughts, and prodromal phase psychosis. Two weeks later, motivated by this training, I asked a failing and visibly unhappy student if she was suicidal. Thankfully she said no, that she was over that now.

Being depressed has not harmed my teaching, though—if anything, it has helped it by bringing me closer to my students. And if working here doesn't make me happy, perhaps that's not the point. It has made me better, and taught me empathy. It has made me less of an idiot by rethinking pedagogy from the ground up, with humility, and from my students' points of view. Serving our community has made me a better citizen, and a better father, and a terrible husband. Yes, the dream of teaching at an intellectually vibrant (liberal arts) college is almost certainly dead, and my academic ambitions died the day I signed. But other dreams I've had—of being a professor, a writer, a chess coach, a half-mensch; of earning tenure and academic freedom; of canceling cable; of cosplaying *Catch-22* and getting paid for it—those dreams have all come true.

II. A Small Rural University

Southeastern Sideways State University is located in Hope City in Cowherd County, Southeast USA. The setting is rural, with long stretches of farmland lining state connector roads. A recent Census of Agriculture counts approximately 370 farms in Cowherd County totaling 160,000 or so acres. Outside of farming, its largest industries are manufacturing, health care, social work, and education. Hope City boasts one large hospital, a Walmart, SSSU, and a local technical college. The public recreational center serves as a community service and child-activity hub, as do a large number of religious institutions. And thank God for those; there is no movie theater, bowling alley, skating rink, arcade, or anything else within 40 minutes of town.

Both Hope City and Cowherd County are socioeconomically underdeveloped and losing residents. I've been called to jury duty three times. In 2022 the city had a population of around 15,600, down from 17,000 in 2010. This mirrors Cowherd County as a whole, whose population was around 28,900 in 2022, down from 32,800 in 2010. The 2021 poverty rate in Cowherd County was around 24 percent. That same year, the median household income was approximately $37,000 and median property value was approximately $117,000, both in annual decline. Cowherd County's education system includes five public schools, plus one state charter school and a K-12 private academy. The state DOE classifies 100 percent of students in the Cowherd County school system as "economically disadvantaged," and a related department indicates 95 percent of all K-12 county students as eligible for free or reduced lunch. Cowherd County proficiency levels for reading in elementary, middle, and high school are 12 percent, 8 percent, and 19 percent, respectively; corresponding numbers in math proficiency are 10 percent, 4 percent, 4 percent. The school system is also bizarrely imbalanced demographically. Where the overall Black, White, and Hispanic percentages of Cowherd County are approximately 53 percent, 44 percent, and 6 percent, respectively, enrollment in the Cowherd County school district is approximately 77 percent Black, 7 percent White, and 13 percent Hispanic. A large number of families, disproportionately White, school their children either out-of-county or at the K-12 academy with 98 percent White enrollment.

This story is not atypical for rural counties in this region, and a significant percentage of SSSU's student body spring from this socioeconomic milieu. The university's fall 2022 total enrollment (graduate and undergraduate) was around 3,000. The racial demographics of that group are approximately 57 percent White, 26 percent African American, 8 percent Asian and Pacific Islander, and 6 percent Hispanic, among others. Approximately 40 percent of undergraduates received Pell Grants, and around half are First-Generation college students. Two-thirds are women. Most SSSU students live close to home: in Fall 2023, approximately 11 percent of students lived in Cowherd County, 28 percent in directly adjacent counties, and another 17 percent or so in counties within one hour's drive. A significant number are nontraditional students—18 percent began college for the first-time at age 25 or older; and 22 percent are age 25 or older. Whether traditional or non-traditional, a large percentage of SSSU students have full-time jobs; and those living close to home typically have family members (whether children, spouses, siblings, parents, or grandparents) to care for. The acceptance rate is between 85 percent and 90 percent. There is no SAT/ACT requirement, but the mid reported SAT range is around 1050–1100. The latest six-year graduation rate for first-time full-time freshmen was approximately 32 percent (compared to 93 percent at a nearby R1).

In a nutshell—most of our students are "at-risk" for one reason or another, if not several. In the classroom this manifests in debilitating academic under-preparation, lack of motivation and study skills, chronic absenteeism, depression, anxiety, and other mental health challenges, apathy about grades, unexplained disappearances, and ineffectual emails from administrators about so-called "early warning" systems that nobody uses. Sometimes by choice, and often by necessity, academic success takes a backseat to work, family, and extracurriculars. Last month I had several students miss class, some of them already failing, because the same administrators emailing about "early warnings" decided they should build a house. The result each semester is a disturbingly high number of withdrawals and non-passing grades—or "high DFW" in committee-speak. At SSSU, this is especially pronounced in freshman courses, and even more so in science and math courses, where students in Fall 2023 either failed or withdrew from classes at the following rates: Essentials of Biology I (58%), Principles of Chemistry I (52%), Intro to Geosciences I (49%), Human Anatomy and Physiology (48%), Quantitative Reasoning (47%), and Pre-calculus (46%). Intro to American Government, which I teach, had an institutional "W+F" percentage of 33 percent.

III. Great Leap Forward

When I joined SSSU almost a decade ago, my teaching experience did not align with this place. I had taught for several years at a highly ranked

R1 in California, and a selective liberal arts college in the northeast. There I could lean (for the most part) on the talent and motivation of my students. I assigned them long and difficult readings, and lots of papers. I showed no mercy on grades. I took their attendance for granted, and held students accountable for bringing their own preparation to lectures. We dove deeply into complicated historical and philosophical issues. We read books. We read Kant and liked it. It was thrilling. I took this as a model of what teaching is, or ought to be. I also took my students to be indicative of who college students are, or ought to be.

SSSU was different. For example, in my American Government course, it was not anomalous for a quarter of my students to miss a quarter of our classes, or for half the class to bomb most of the tests, many not even attempting the essay questions. But despite regularly failing a third of the class, student pushback was rare. As long as I didn't scold them, they accepted pretty much anything. My emotional response to this situation shifted erratically each week; from bewilderment and concern on Monday, to frustration and anger on Tuesday, to total dissociation by Friday. I blamed the students. "They should work harder. They should care more. They should study more. They should come to class. They shouldn't be here at all. I'm a teacher, not a social worker." This got me nowhere. It didn't help me cope, and it certainly didn't help me teach.

What did help was the support of my colleagues. SSSU has an infrastructure that encourages and incentivizes meaningful faculty engagement about teaching. These include a variety of faculty-led "Faculty Learning Communities" (FLCs) that pay around $300 for attending three to six meetings and, at the conclusion, providing some artifact of its impact in the classroom. I have attended too many of these to count, covering topics like "Transparency in Learning and Teaching" (TILT), "Teaching Gen Z," and "Integrating ePorfolios," or trendy books like Ken Bain's *What the Best College Teachers Do* (2004), James Barber's *Facilitating the Integration of Learning* (2020), and James Lang's *Small Teaching* (2016). I cannot hyperbolize the impact of these FLC's on my morale, outlook, and teaching.

First, they introduced me to practically every faculty member on campus. From day one, I wasn't left on an island. And my colleagues' participation culturally reinforced the importance of teaching, and teaching well. Even if no one applied this stuff in their classes, the existence of these learning communities made continual pedagogical improvement *seem* like a norm. Second, they provided a necessary space for sharing, empathizing, venting, and laughing. Inevitably these meetings degenerate into a game of one-upmanship for the most bizarre classroom story—like when a student showed up late to class, grabbed a stranger's water bottle, started drinking from it, and then sat down like nothing happened; or when a student emailed, concerned that "they are a 4.0 student" but needed alternative study materials because they "have never learned much from reading"; or how advising a student was hard because he wouldn't meet in person, refused to activate his phone camera, and when he finally did, pressed the camera to his forehead; or how all of us were missing students throughout the week due to a "university sanctioned" trophy event.

Most importantly, the FLCs improved my teaching. At first it all seemed gimmicky, a load of buzzwords—like "high-impact practices," TILT, integrative learning, reacting to the past, student-centered teaching, mindset, mindthink, groupthink, nothink. It felt like ideology, language for those who fancied themselves "good teachers" by being nice and lowering standards. Sure, I'll attend the meetings, and I'll collect the money. I'll even add a "reflection" piece where students can ramble on about anything except the course material, if that's what you want. And I did. But here's the thing—the more "transparent" assignments I created, the more "reflection" pieces I read, and the more seriously I went about making coursework "student-centered," the better my courses actually got, and the better my students performed, and the better I felt about things.

One example occurred in American Government, where I created an end-of-course "Career Relevance Paper" that required students to tell me their major, how that relates to their career goals, and three ways the course related to that career. They could link it to the Bill of Rights and civil rights, Congressional laws, Supreme Court decisions, parties and interest groups, local vs. federal, bureaucracy, you name it. Anything works, easy A. I was stunned by the results—contrary to my beliefs, most students had some idea of why they were here, and what career they wanted. In general terms: aspiring business owners might talk about how non-discrimination and disability laws or OSHA might impact their business; nursing majors might mention how CDC policy or Obamacare impacts their workplace; art majors can discuss the First Amendment, etc. The assignment generally helps students make these connections. In practice, it also helped me better understand—and appreciate—who they were, and why they were here. It made them more human.

Another example occurred in Constitutional Law. My first-year syllabus covered the textbook cases, and the students could not have cared less. I then went to these FLCs on "student-centered teaching," and they hammered the idea of finding materials that students can relate to. So I did—I scrapped the classics and loaded the course with cases on free speech and civil rights in K-12 and college environments. These cases were new to me, and I learned a lot from the prep. And the response from students was immediate. On First Amendment principles we debated the recognition of controversial student organizations, watched videos of campus protests, viewed censored college newspapers, and discussed our campus's Christmas-themed programming. Student government representatives in the class related our case studies to issues they had tackled throughout that year. I pressed them with hard hypotheticals. Our class activities were engaging. Students overcame stage fright and participated. Grades went up. Maybe two did the readings.

I could cite many more examples, but I take the larger lesson of these FLCs to be what one colleague calls "the power of friendship," something that manifests in genuine empathy among faculty, in unironic sharing and criticism of ideas, and in sincere encouragement to try new things. And in $300. This in turn leads to productive classes and a better experience for students. I still don't have it in me to try Reacting to the Past in my own classes—but I'll be damned if I haven't pretended to be a self-flagellating Catholic priest in a plague-infested 14th-century British town in someone else's class, and loved every minute of it.

IV. Catch-22

"Hello?"

"Hi, Professor, this is Y—n!"

"Y—n! Hi, how are you doing? Nice to hear from you! How's life after graduation?"

"I'm doing great, how are you?"

"I'm fine—you know, teaching over summer, trying to research while I can. What's up?"

"Well, I'm calling, actually, because I am applying for jobs, and I just got an interview for a position at _____. I appreciate all the help you've given me. And since you were my advisor and professor, I was wondering if you would be willing to serve as a reference?"

"Sure, I'd be happy to, but there's a Catch."

"What catch?"

"Anything I say will be the truth, the whole truth, and nothing but the truth."

"What do you mean?"

"I mean I'm happy to take a call or write a letter, but I'm going to tell the truth."

"Okay. So what does that mean?"

"It means what I just said. Remember all those times I told you that this university is not the real world? You didn't believe me, but now the chickens are coming home. In the real world, how many chances do you get to disappear from your job without notice for weeks at a time, or to ignore submission deadlines? One month ago, I was your advisor, and your professor. It was my job to do anything possible to help you graduate. But what did I tell you every time you made me jump through hoops, or pushed me to the brink of my ethics? 'Promise you won't draw the wrong conclusion,' I said. Because this place isn't the real world. It's the land of Oz. It's the wizard behind the curtain. It's the bizarro world, a Catch-22 world. In here you are a valued customer. You pay the institution to be here, and it wants you to pa.... I mean stay, as long as possible. If you fail every class, it will put you on 'supported enrollment' and make you a residence hall leader. If you can't pass math, they'll make someone else teach it. Fifth grade—that's what you want to teach? Well then that's all the math you need. Sixth grade math ain't got nothin' to do with your future. But let me ask you this—what happens when all that monopoly money you're getting from financial aid runs out? What happens when you can't pass go and collect ten more thousand dollars that ain't yours anyway? That's when Toto pulls the curtain, and they send you back to Kansas. Now it's Catch-22. You want a job? Now *they* are paying *you* to be there. Now *you* are the product—and what do you have to show them? It better be more than a thin sheet of paper with your name on it, because they won't tolerate that nonsense we tolerated here; no, sir, not unless you've got some financial aid package I don't know about that can pay you to work for them. And they don't want nonsense from me, either. By waiving all the rules, I served you well, didn't I? But I didn't serve them. In the real world my good name and my word still have to mean something. And whatever I covered up in here, I can't cover it up out there. That's what I've been trying to tell you. I care about you, and right now I'm disappointing you. But this is my final lesson, maybe the most important lesson of all. It's Catch-22, Y—n. Now it's the truth, the whole truth, and nothing but the truth. If you can accept that and live with that, then give them my name, and I'm here for you."

"Ok, thanks. I'll probably ask someone else, then."

V. Friends of the Ayatollah

The Iranian hostage crisis lasted 444 days. With a month left in the academic year, my colleague begins a countdown. "They're fueling the jets," he says after Spring Break. "They're taking off the blindfolds," he says during finals week. "Reagan just took office, and the Ayatollah gave Carter the finger on his way out." That must mean grades were submitted.

A major breakthrough in my teaching came when I realized that pretty much everyone here feels like a hostage. Hell, even the President was dying to leave. And so I thought, while we're all trapped here together for four months at a time, why not learn about each other, and find new ways to help each other? And so I started doing studies. I took the strategies from the FLCs—like Transparency in Teaching and Learning, High-Impact Practices, and Integrative Learning—and designed simple and measurable interventions for my assignments, tests, and study guides. I got IRB approval. I offered students extra credit to complete pre- and post-tests and surveys. I taught myself caveman statistics. I started leading my own FLCs and worked closely with an inspirational, perfect-person of a colleague to host scholarship workshops, share my data, and encourage others to join. They did. We published an edited journal volume of our work. I learned that replacing words like "deleterious," "equalized," "preceded," and "subordinate" with smaller words boosted my students' scores a lot. I would now write much better, and fairer, tests for them.

I do this every semester now. One of the anxieties of working at a rural state university, where we regularly teach 4–4 or 5–5 schedules with exorbitant service requirements, is that finding time to write and publish is difficult. Realizing how much I could learn about how my *students* learn through careful empirical research, and how many venues existed to publish this research if done well, ultimately gave new purpose and impetus to my teaching. Now, as I teach students about government, or philosophy, or revolutions, or whatever, I'm also learning about them. And the more I learn about them, the more I understand them, the better I can teach them.

What I have learned above all is to embrace our students unconditionally, to "meet them where they are." And so that's why, next year, the Ayatollah and me are collaborating on a project to give students credit for missing class. It's a win-win—the more classes they miss, the more credit we'll give them for missing, and the more data we'll have to work with. You want flexibility? You can miss every single class. But there's a Catch—to receive credit for any absence you must document, in an ePortfolio, the specific reasons behind it. And you must periodically reflect on that record—on your challenges and priorities, your dreams and actions, and your performance in the class—and be able to tell a story about it. No matter how arbitrary or legitimate—hating the professor counts just as much as jury duty—all we want is an honest record and a sincere reflection. Truth, the whole truth, and nothing but the truth. For once in their lives, that's how they'll be judged. Telling the truth is worth an A. And at semester's end we'll read their stories—of work and family, illness and death, despair and regret, pressure and pain, apathy, anxiety, and absurdity; and in this bizarro classroom, in this Sideways school, we may finally come to know and appreciate our students for who they are, and for where college fits into their lives.

VI. A Ticket to Anywhere

Friedrich transferred to SSSU after leaving a highly ranked research university elsewhere in the state. At SSSU this profile invariably means three things—first, he is a super talented student; second, a crisis of some sort—personal, financial, mental, or familial—derailed his education; and third, he lives in or around Hope City. I was Friedrich's advisor—check, check, and check. He took several of my classes, and regularly produced some of the most thoughtful and interesting work that I have read at SSSU. Unfortunately, he almost always submitted it late, and would disappear from class for weeks at a time. Based solely on the quality of work, he should have graduated Magna or Summa. But absences and late penalties took their toll, and it boiled down to survival.

Friedrich and I spoke regularly in my office about life and politics, the Supreme Court, and Karl Marx. He was thoughtful and self-aware. He had a worldview that was well-defined, but not lacking in humility. He cared about the state of the world, and more often than not, seemed troubled by it. He was also prone to bouts of depression and loneliness, which I suspect derailed his first attempt at college. In sum, through our conversations I discovered a person of immense character, and a wealth of talent, but inhibited by a lack of confidence, little direction, and, perhaps most critically, a dead-end job as a hotel desk manager that he hated, but would never quit. As chance would have it, Friedrich became friends with my father, who would regularly stay at Friedrich's hotel during family visits. Once Friedrich almost seemed proud to tell me that they had chatted over a smoke break. He would ask about my dad, and my dad would ask about him. When my father died unexpectedly of brain cancer, I received Friedrich's sincere condolence.

Our relationship changed after graduation. Once every couple months I would get a call from Friedrich. He would ask me about the Supreme Court's abortion ruling, or about the January 6 riot—just checking in, a reason to talk. Other times he would call in serious distress—about unhealthy relationships, or unhappiness at work, or general anxiety. On a couple occasions, when it was clear to me that his state of mind was unhealthy, if not dangerous, I asked him to seek more effective help. No matter what the occasion, though, I repeatedly told him to do one thing—get the hell out of here. Pick a city on the map where you want to live, buy a plane ticket, and go. I said this to him every time we talked for at least three years—just go ... anywhere. And to be sure, he tried. I wrote several recommendations for AmeriCorps and PeaceCorps. He eventually took one opportunity to teach underserved students in St. Louis. It was good, but short lived. And then he was right back, working in the same hotel, again hating every minute of it.

I hadn't heard from Friedrich for a while. Then one day I got a call. "Professor Young!" he said. "How are you doing?" I knew it was him, but he sounded different. "Friedrich," I said, "I'm great, how are you? What are you doing? Where are you?" And then he said something I will never forget: "I'm in San Diego! I've been here for two weeks and I've already gotten three job interviews!" I could barely believe my ears. "What are you doing there? How did you get there?" I asked. "I met someone on Facebook," he said. "They invited me here, and so I just said what the hell and bought a plane ticket, and now I'm here, and it's the best thing I ever did."

He said he couldn't believe how many doors had opened simply by moving to a bigger city, and how he had taken difficult steps—like giving up alcohol for good—to improve his life. And how great the weather was. And how happy he was to be there. And how I should visit San Diego. And would I write him a letter? And I told him how proud I was of him for buying that ticket, and taking control of his life, and having the courage to follow his heart and leave this place. Not everyone has that courage. They stay here forever, marching towards death, leading lives of quiet desperation. Not Friedrich. It's been a year since he left. He hasn't called me since.

I Quit
When the Tenure Track Is a Dead End

Kathryn D. Blanchard

Picture this: it's 2005, and you're a fifth-year Ph.D. student in theology and ethics at a fancy university in a small city, putting yourself on the job market even though your dissertation isn't done. "Just for practice," you tell yourself. "It'll be ok if I don't get one this year."

Looking at job openings makes you anxious. Religious studies is a weird animal, and you realize you might have backed yourself into a corner with the sub-specialty you chose. You are not a fit in temperament for religious schools (mostly Catholic or evangelical) that want someone to toe the theological line. And you are also not a fit on paper for secular schools that don't want weird religious Christians in their departments. What you really want is a generalist position in religious studies at a liberal arts college, and these are few and far between.

You send out a couple dozen applications anyway. Miraculously, you get two conference interviews in the fall—one for a specialist position at a university divinity school that everyone has heard of in the northeast, and one for a generalist position at an undergraduate college no one has heard of in the Midwest. The northeastern school thanks you for your time; the midwestern school, loosely affiliated with the mainline religious denomination you currently call yours, invites you to campus in the winter. After what seems like a good day and a half of interviews, followed by weeks of painful waiting, the offer comes in the spring of 2006.

You got a tenure-track job on your first try! Despite your weird dissertation! All your years of work and humiliation have paid off! You're unstoppable!

"Are you going to take it?" your dad asks, because he has spent his career in the business world, where options for educated white men always abound. Some of your grad school colleagues ask the same thing, because they've never heard of that college, and they have their hearts set on jobs that will let them teach two or three courses a year to graduate students in their specialty, while spending most of their time gaining renown through research and publishing. You're pretty sure such a job does not exist for you. You feel beyond lucky to have a single offer.

"Of course I'm going to take it," you say. "It's a tenure-track job at a liberal arts college." You just spent five years in grad school (plus three years before that in seminary) for precisely this, and you feel great about it. You loved being an undergraduate student, and you are excited to teach undergraduates. And even though you like research and writing, you never expected to become a well-known scholar. You enjoy the wide variety in your discipline and are excited about the opportunity to teach stuff you don't already know, meaning you can stay in learning mode for the rest of your life. You do not feel this job is beneath you.

So you move your little family (spouse, toddler, two cats) eight hundred miles away to a small rural town, 140 miles from the nearest airport hub. While you're moving into your new office, the guy whose office it used to be, whom you replaced, stops by to meet you. You find out he worked there for thirty-five years. You asked if he liked it. "Yeah," he says, "in the first few years when I could have still gotten out."

Damn. You shake it off, chalking this up to his own personality defect.

You manage to finish and defend your dissertation just weeks before you teach your first class as a *Real Professor*. Your first few years as a teacher include some significant missteps, but you hang in there with a lot of help from friends and mentors, and eventually find your rhythm, learning how to work with these particular students in this particular place. You'll never be the most popular teacher on campus, but your classes are always full, thanks largely to humanities distributive requirements. Students generally report learning interesting new things in your classes, with only moderate suffering, and a handful of them come back for more, even to the point of majoring or minoring in religious studies.

But—and there's always a but—there are other parts of being a faculty member that make the job less fun. The 2008 market crash hits the endowment, enrollment, and teacher salaries hard, such that crisis mode becomes the norm. There are colleagues who behave badly, especially toward younger women with little power to push back. You spend thankless hours in committees and task forces that don't effect any meaningful change. Your spouse is unhappy living in a small town with few job prospects. You live far away from all the people in the world who love you, and it's been harder to make friends with a family in tow.

So pretty soon you try to move on, applying for jobs near cities, year after year, almost like a hobby. It should be easier to get a job now, you think; you have a few years of experience under your belt, along with some publications. But the same problem you had before—weird subdiscipline in a shrinking humanities field—is even more acute than it was before the market crash. You get a few first interviews but no second interviews, because now you're competing with newer, shinier people.

Meanwhile, in your fifth year you get tenure. Job security! You can keep this job till you're old and grey! (As long as you're not stupid enough to say or do something truly illegal.)

But—here's another but that no one talks about—the flip side of security is being stuck.

Job interviews come to a grinding halt. Absolutely no one is looking to hire an associate professor. To avoid giving into boredom, you look for new challenges to keep yourself engaged. You go to conferences and write more things. You try your hand at public scholarship. (Never read the comments.) You get trained to do peer evaluation visits with your regional accreditation body. You join committees and task forces for tenured folks. You develop new classes. You get a dog. You look forward to summers with family. You try to appreciate the work-life balance that your job affords you—this job that you can now mostly do with one hand tied behind your back.

You know how grateful you should be, in this industry full of contingency, and you feel guilty for complaining. You are mindful of all the people piecing together part-time adjunct gigs who would kill for your job, and you try to practice solidarity with all people everywhere who feel stuck in jobs they don't love or even like. *Why can't I just treat this like a job like any other job?* you ask yourself. *Why can't I just do my best and be satisfied?*

Time keeps passing. You go up for full professor a year early, mainly because it's the only way to get a salary bump. After a year as full professor, you are shocked to receive an endowed chair—which comes with a much bigger salary bump (though your salary is still laughable by most professional standards). There is now literally nowhere else for you to go as a faculty member at this institution. You decide to get a new credential, an MBA, in hopes that it will open doors—either to new endeavors at your college, or to jobs at other institutions. Maybe it worked. Hiring committees seem to find your resume interesting again, and you start getting a few interviews for administrative positions like dean or division chair or associate provost or director.

And then: a pandemic. You learn how to use a new learning management system and how to teach online, or masked in person. You do your best to support students whose faces you have never seen and whose names you have trouble learning. You fight for your administrators to care about staff and faculty health, but they don't listen. They can't afford to listen, you see. The school is not wealthy enough or famous enough to absorb a year with no students on campus. You *will* teach, they tell you, and you will teach *in person*, and you will do whatever you can to help us retain students, because if the students leave, you'll lose your job anyway.

In addition, your institution decides the pandemic is a good time to make big program cuts—including the religious studies major. You—the only religious studies professor left—aren't being fired, but you will no longer teach any upper-level courses. You will teach first-year seminars, introductory courses, and one-offs to students for whom your class is something to "get out of the way" before majoring in business or pre-health fields. You may still manage to hook a few of them enough to take a second course, and maybe they'll even pull together a minor. But the days are gone when you can expect anyone to prioritize the thing for which you exist professionally.

And that's the last straw. You realize you're done. You have nothing left to give to this job. You've exhausted all your creativity in finding ways to keep this job interesting and engaging and meaningful, but it was apparently for naught. You're out of ideas. After fifteen years, you find you have become dead weight on the faculty—the party of no, the person who always sees why some great new idea will never work.

You are toxic sludge, and you must go.

So you quit, as graciously as possible, joining what will be known as the "great resignation." There is no job waiting for you in the wings. Your safety net is your savings, and your faith that you can find some work once you get where you're going. Your kid flies the nest, and you and your spouse (plus dog and three different cats) move 500 miles to be near your elderly parents. You sell your house to the college's new religious studies professor, who is young and idealistic like you used to be. You try not to rain on his parade like your predecessor did to you.

Fast forward three years, much of which you spent in the gig economy—writing copy for advertising, doing odd consulting gigs, and giving tours at a whiskey distillery. You also wrote a novel, not yet published. You applied for many more jobs in academia and the nonprofit sector, some in your new city, some remote, all of which ended in rejection. The job you finally got—as a secretary in a government office—came out of left field, thanks to the friend of a friend. It has nothing to do with your education or anything in your past career, but it gives you a regular schedule, steady income, health insurance for your family, and time to spend with your parents.

Some of your academic friends and acquaintances seem frankly horrified to hear that you are a secretary. They look at you with pity. They want to know if your co-workers are aware of how much education you have, or if they call you Doctor. They don't seem to believe you when you tell them you are happy doing this job that is mostly answering phones and making sure information ends up in appropriate places. But you're genuinely satisfied making a small contribution, simply by doing your best. It is relatively low stress, and the people around you are kind and glad you're there. You're learning a new industry, and you enjoy being helpful to your coworkers and the citizens whose taxes pay your salary. And—perhaps most intriguing—there is the possibility of advancement. Your new boss knows the landscape well and promises to support your future career (for however long that might be, given your advancing age). It is not a dead end. You are not stuck.

You wonder why you could never seem to reach this level of satisfaction as a tenured professor, which was still pretty bad pay but at least came with a flexible schedule, long vacations, lots of good people, an office door that closed, and even a modicum of respect. Was a steady state really so bad?

You decide your dissatisfaction had something to do with your own expectations: being a professor was a "vocation" and even an identity to you, rather than a "job." There is a good deal less self-importance in having a secretarial job (even though such jobs are crucial to most collective human endeavors). You are not on a mission. You do not expect it to be "meaningful" in the way you wanted being a professor to be. Your work enables *other people's* meaningful work. Your identity now comes from the other parts of your life: being a daughter, wife, mother, friend, citizen, neighbor, and—very occasionally—a former professor.

On Not Getting Tenure

G. Thomas Couser

The attainment of tenure has become rarer and rarer. Over the last fifty or so years, the ratio of tenured to untenured appointments has been effectively reversed, so that today about three-quarters of faculty appointments are off the tenure track. While I support tenure in principle—the principle of protecting academic freedom, which seems to be increasingly imperiled today—I realize that it is, for too many, an inaccessible status. So the divide between the haves and the have-nots has become sharper and more troubling than when I entered the profession in 1976.

* * *

In 1981, I was denied tenure at Connecticut College, a small liberal arts college. During the following year, I wrote an essay to express my reaction to what seemed a personal and professional catastrophe. I submitted it to several journals and quarterlies, such as *American Scholar* and *College English*, without success. It reads as follows:

> There are subtler ways of dissecting the academic world, but none simpler and truer than to bisect its population between those who have tenure and those who don't. Peculiar to that world, the tenure system is not well understood or widely appreciated outside it; indeed, it is under increasing criticism within it. But while the system may be controversial, it is apparently not dispensable: through it, the academy defines and protects its highest values, the vigorous pursuit and free expression of the truth, and through the tenure review, academic institutions literally constitute themselves, by selecting their permanent members. The binary division into haves and have-nots is, and is likely to remain, at the heart of academic life because the tenure principle is the informal constitution of the academic world.
>
> The institution is controversial today because economic circumstances have greatly increased the stakes; while the differences among candidates for tenure may be minor, the consequences of the tenure decision are major. Those who get tenure enjoy virtually absolute job security—and academic freedom—until

retirement. Those who don't—more than half of those who are reviewed—may seek tenure elsewhere, but many are forced to leave the profession—this, after they have devoted a dozen or so years to graduate work and teaching. I am reminded of Red Sox pitcher Bill Lee's comment after he lost a close but crucial game to the [Cincinnati] Reds' Don Gullett in the 1975 World Series: "He's going to the Hall of Fame, and I'm going to the Eliot Lounge" [a local bar]. It is the drastic difference between the fates of the winners and losers, the haves and have-nots, the elect and the damned, that gives the tenure system its troubling implications today. Always an important annual ritual, the granting of tenure is becoming a kind of ritual sacrifice to the gods of academe. As one of the recent sacrificial victims, I would like to comment on the professional and institutional implications of the system. But first, I would like to explore its personal implications, to explain what not getting tenure is like.

I came up for tenure in a very top-heavy department in a small liberal arts college that, until recently, gave tenure quite liberally. The cost of that liberality has been a sudden and severe escalation in the standards for tenure: the cost of that escalation will be the decimation of a generation of talented teaching scholars. The year before I came up for tenure was the year of the first tenure slaughter. Of five candidates, only one was tenured; of the four denied tenure, only one remains in the academy. The rest have chosen not to gamble another five years on the tenure slot machine. [Had I been granted tenure, the English Department would have been "tenured up"; all of the members would have tenure—an administrator's nightmare.] So I knew from the beginning of the review that, however well I had performed, it might not be well enough.

In retrospect, it seems as though I spent the entire fall fussing with my tenure file—trying to condense my five years in the profession into a folder full of paper; the entire winter fighting anxiety—trying not to read too much into overheard remarks and casual campus encounters, and the entire spring warding off the depression caused by an administrative decision not to tenure me—and writing a lengthy brief in the hope of reversing the decision. I must have done other things; of course I had to teach, and I did so, somehow. But the review does consume nearly a whole academic year, and it is easy to become self-absorbed. I knew I was obsessed when one day I misheard the innocent modifier "ten-year" as the watchword, "tenure." Long-distance running, once recreation, became therapy; day after day I'd pound out my frustration on the pavement, restoring an equilibrium that would enable me to work.

In the end, I came tantalizingly close to getting tenure; my department and the faculty advisory committee recommended me, but the college president overruled them. Coming close is scant solace; the decision remains a fundamental and final rejection by the institution I had courted for half a decade. As it happened, I received the news, in the form of a letter from the president, a week or so earlier than I had expected it. For the better part of a year, I had imagined or mentally rehearsed various reactions to the possible outcomes; while I knew that I could neither predict nor control my response, I had at least planned to brace for the news. In spite of the fact that my guard was down on what proved to be the crucial day, I did not faint, as I thought I might if the news was bad, nor did I go out and get drunk or go home to cry. The decision registered only remotely at first; I didn't, or couldn't, assimilate it fully.

Numbed, I went to lunch as usual, shared the news with some friends, and joked feebly about it; they consoled me and urged me to appeal the decision. What I remember feeling was not a rush of emotion but the sense that I had been suddenly and subtly, but profoundly and irrevocably, changed. In retrospect, I see myself at that moment as the cartoon character who has stepped off a cliff, and knows it, but has not yet begun to fall; the bottom had fallen out of my world but gravity—the gravity of my predicament—had not yet taken effect. After lunch I taught my afternoon class. I was secretly proud of my self-control; at the same time, I knew I desperately needed what teaching, like sleeping, can provide—the total obliteration of other concerns. I retreated, then, to the place from which I was to be, in effect, expelled, and while that class did provide fifty minutes of respite, I felt somehow distanced from myself as well as from my students; I was on autopilot. I felt disembodied, like a ghost of myself.

Once the news did register, I was overwhelmed by emotions that have only gradually faded. Like a bereavement, not getting tenure haunts you all day every day, at first. Soon after awakening, you remember the unpleasant fact, little things remind you of it all day, and it's likely to be the last thing you think of at night. The allusion to death is not accidental. Not getting tenure, I feel sure, must be in some way like learning you are going to die soon. I say this not because denial of tenure makes one's appointment, in administrative language "terminal," although I see a grim joke in that term now. I say it because one feels unfairly singled out for an unhappy, unavoidable, and premature fate. From reading about and witnessing the predicament of the terminally ill, I gather that denial of tenure generates many of the same responses on a smaller scale: sorrow, anger, denial, envy, resignation. Despite the neatness of analyses of grief, these reactions do not come in predictable or progressive sequences, either. The volatility of one's emotions is as threatening as their power.

The experience has another similarity with that of suffering terminal illness: no one really wants to talk about it with you. Your affliction, while not catching, is distressing to those around you, for different reasons. Those who made the decision are understandably uneasy with your pain. Those who got tenure in earlier years may feel defensive because standards were lower then. Those who haven't yet come up for tenure are torn in several directions: they may be stunned at what the decision implies about current standards, hopeful that your not getting tenure may make room for them, sympathetic toward your plight, resolved that it should not become their fate, and terrified that it may. Those who got tenure when you didn't—the more sensitive among them, at least—experience a combination of relief, pity, and survivors' guilt. Most colleagues are supportive, but they often express their concern indirectly. They shake their heads and mutter about the tragic waste of talent and ask your close friends discreetly, "how's he taking it?" Clearly, the whole community agonizes over the annual ritual, but finally you suffer alone.

It dawned on me one day, as I groped for ways to assimilate this novel and unwelcome experience, that it must be like getting fired. But that revelation soon led to its own correction: it wasn't *like* getting fired, it *was* getting fired. That event is probably traumatic in any circumstances; one hears of employees—executives, even—told to clear out their desks by the end of the workday. But in the academy, the process has a deceptive civility; you are given a generous period in which to find a new job, and the terminating letter may have all the tact of a Dear John letter. What is insidious about this gentility is, in part, its emptiness; even a generous amount of time may not turn up a job within the profession. In part, it's that the lame-duck period is inherently painful. Like the terminally ill, you continue to live in the world that is soon to exclude you. You do the same things you've been doing, but now plagued by envy of those whose future is longer than yours. As the terminally ill often are, you are outwardly the same, but your status has changed decisively and irreversibly—and everyone knows it. While you are not stigmatized, you may succumb to a sense of shame. And while you are not ostracized, you cease to matter very much. Your advice is sought less frequently; colleagues begin to think of you—and even speak of you—in the past tense. The disengagement is mutual. You permit yourself to drop the unpleasant duties all faculty members complain about; you may skip faculty and department meetings, resign from committees, keep shorter office hours. You find yourself with more time for what you consider your central tasks—reading, writing, and teaching—but these may now seem pointless.

The most troubling aspect of not getting tenure may be the nagging suspicion that you've been treated unjustly; the dominant, perhaps residual, emotion, is anger. This is because being up for tenure is rather like being on trial. This analogy was suggested by others: when I tried to explain to a nonacademic friend the nature and purpose of the long probationary period, his astonished response was, "Six years in the institution? That's not probation, that's a prison term." Beyond the linguistic overlap—I've become used to talking of probation, review, evidence, and appeal—is the essential similarity: one's fate is being judged by others on limited, sometimes unreliable, evidence. Unfortunately, in an economy that forces administrators to rationalize decisions often dictated by the market, the burden of proof is very much on the candidate for tenure; he is presumed guilty (unworthy) until he proves himself innocent. I used to joke that the tenure review was such an ordeal that it made you feel you deserved tenure just for enduring it. The joke no longer seems funny to me; rather, it seems to reveal a sad truth: these days the competition is such that many people who deserve tenure won't get it, ever. This helps to resolve the paradox of my perception of the tenure review; while I have no reason to *think* it was unfair, I *feel* that it was. That is, I can't point to any procedural error or manifest prejudice in the handling of my case—or I would sue—but I still feel that I have been done an injustice.

For the first time in what may have been a sheltered life, then, I have experienced something that simply feels wrong and that I am unable to right. I know now how powerful a sense of injustice can be; in me, it has generated an anger I find difficult to express, let alone transcend. As a result, I think I better understand people of whom it is said that a single experience soured them on life. But while I have come to appreciate the power of a sense of injustice, I also understand that a sense of injustice is a subjective phenomenon that may not always be rooted in an objective act or state of injustice. I think my experience has given me a general insight into the trial process: when complex truths have to be resolved in binary choices, the results are unlikely to seem fair to all parties. If justice is as elusive as my experience suggests, my sympathy extends to those who are charged with achieving it as well as those on trial.

It helps to note, too, that the undeniable intensity and apparent inequity of the tenure review derive ultimately from hard demographic facts. Facing an uncertain future as the number of college-age youth declines steeply in the next decade, college administrators are naturally reluctant to tenure anyone. It's safer and cheaper to fire and hire. So standards for tenure rise sharply as—and because—the size of the applicant pool decreases. Those coming up for tenure today are caught in a demographic double-bind: they are members of the baby-boom generation in the profession that stands to suffer most from the baby bust.

It helps somewhat to know that demography, rather than some hostile colleagues or benighted administrator, is the villain, for the tenure review is a process that breeds suspicion. In my case, suspicion became paranoia when I misplaced my elaborate appeal file just before it was due. Rather than conduct the methodical search of my office that would have turned it up, I panicked and became convinced that someone—a jealous colleague, hostile student, or malevolent administrator—had stolen it. My madness had a certain logic. One colleague had already read my brief without my permission; why shouldn't another take it without permission, perhaps to destroy it? I had been denied tenure; therefore, I had enemies. The next day, finding it buried under another file, I could laugh at the elaborate scenarios I had constructed to account for simple absent-mindedness; even now, it embarrasses me to confess it. But the episode illustrates how powerfully the mind seeks to blame proximate human agents. Self-righteousness can be seductive. But it's healthier to view the event in its proper, demographic context, to understand that one's advancement in the profession may have less to do with one's worth and more and more to do with luck and timing.

Next to anger, the most debilitating emotion generated by not getting tenure is depression. The depression, which threatens to become hopelessness, stems, I think, from another paradox in not getting tenure; those who don't get tenure are successes who fail. Not getting tenure is usually the first professional setback for those to whom it happens. They have succeeded in getting admitted to topnotch graduate schools, in getting the doctorate, and in getting the most desirable appointments, tenure-track jobs. Because they are accustomed to success, the failure to get tenure can be especially demoralizing; the unfamiliarity of the experience compounds its unpleasantness. Furthermore, to the extent that one's identity is bound up with one's professional role, one's very identity is threatened. Failure may be the last taboo subject in our society. Certainly, one doesn't report going bankrupt or getting divorced—or not getting tenure—to the class notes of one's alumni magazine. Indeed, my main hesitation about writing this essay had to do with the fact that it meant not merely acknowledging, but advertising, a personal failure. I have gone ahead not out of courage and candor but in the conviction that simple judgments of success and failure are arbitrary, external, and irrelevant.

In my essay, I went on to discuss aspects of the tenure review that make it problematic—its reliance on student opinion, its vulnerability to various biases, the pressure on young faculty to publish quickly, the incentive for the untenured to get along by going along, the bitterness of those denied tenure, the loss of their talent to academia, and so on.

It ended this way:

> This may sound like my valedictory to the academic world, but I hope it isn't. I hope to continue my academic career. And even—perhaps, eventually—to get tenure.

During my terminal year, I applied for every job that seemed remotely appropriate, some of which were remote from New England, where I had lived most of my life and hoped to remain. I obtained several interviews at the annual MLA convention (aka the meat market), one campus visit (at a large midwestern university), but not a single offer. (When I landed at LaGuardia upon my return from the midwestern campus, I felt like kneeling to kiss the tarmac, an urge I'd never before experienced.) I was beginning to seriously explore alternative careers and had returned to my doctorate-granting university to take a vocational aptitude test, when the April MLA job-list appeared; in it, Hofstra University advertised an unheard-of *five* full-time lines. My application netted me a campus interview, and after I taught my final class at Connecticut College, Hofstra offered me a job, which of course I accepted. There, after an abbreviated probationary period, and considerable anxiety, I was finally granted tenure in 1986, at the age of forty. As it happened, then, I was one of the lucky ones who survived tenure denial to get another full-time tenure-track job and tenure itself. So, reader, *my* story has a happy ending, and I have been grateful ever since to Hofstra for giving me the second chance that many never got.

Nevertheless, the experience of being denied tenure has long haunted me. The worst aspect of that has been residual resentment of those who voted against me. Although votes are secret and committee members' letters are confidential (at least initially), they may be revealed in the appeal process. (In any case, in a small department, like mine, votes are easy to infer without evidence.) So I soon knew who my "enemies" were. And any contact with them immediately became fraught with anxiety and anger. I remember one day seeing the president (who had the final say in my case) crossing the road in front of my car. I did not try to run him down, but I did maintain enough speed to cause him to hasten his stride a bit. And whenever I encountered him on campus, I made no attempt to disguise my hostility. The same with departmental colleagues I knew had voted against me. I was simmering all the time.

My smoldering resentment became frighteningly clear to me many years later, in 2010, when Amy Bishop, a neurobiologist who'd been denied tenure at the University of Alabama, pulled a handgun out of her purse at a department meeting and shot six of her colleagues, three fatally. While I was shocked and appalled by her actions, I understood the urge; I'd had such fantasies myself. I like to think that Bishop's acting out of my impulse awakened me to the perversity of my fantasy and helped to assuage my anger—as though her act was cathartic for me. Still, to this day, I keep a mental list of my enemies and check them off as they die. And I suspect that I am not alone, or even unusual, in harboring anger for decades after the fateful decision.

The denial also had what I consider a positive effect on my subsequent life in the academy. Serving on tenure committees was the one perk of tenure that I never desired before I obtained it or relished after I did. While it isn't compulsory to serve on tenure committees, it is considered an important service—it's a lot of work—and I dutifully, if reluctantly, served on many over the rest of my career. After all, if one knows the outcome can be unjust, the ethical thing to do is to participate and try to ensure that it is fair. In my service on such committees, I have seen much pettiness—it brings out the worst in some individuals—and I remain wary of it. But if my denial of tenure had one benign effect on me, it was to sensitize me to the trauma of tenure denial. Never wishing it on anyone, I have been very reluctant to vote negatively. I have always been inclined to give candidates the benefit of the doubt.

Of course, for one reason or another, departments do sometimes hire individuals who will not deserve tenure. If their colleagues don't decide against them, administrators will. I've come to think that if colleagues are performing poorly, it is unfair to reappoint them repeatedly for the full probationary period, at least without express reservations. It may be more humane to terminate them early and hope that they find a better venue in which to pursue tenure or leave the profession before investing too much in it.

Teaching Writing in Prison

Nancy Mack

I had resigned my position as a junior high school teacher to stay home with a new baby. After a year of breast-feeding and diaper changing, I started to resemble a zombie living in a bathrobe. I needed to get back to teaching. With only a few weeks before fall term, I applied for a teaching assistantship from Ohio State where I was taking courses for a Ph.D. The only position available was teaching writing courses at a branch campus and in a male prison. I loved teaching junior high students and welcomed the challenge of motivating a different population of reluctant writers. I had attended an inner-city school and believed that I was somewhat street wise. However, I soon found out that I had much to learn from the inmates. My willingness to teach in prison later helped me land a tenure-track job at a small university that was keeping itself afloat with two large prison programs. As a place-bound, first-generation, working-class female in the late seventies, I was highly unlikely to get a tenure-track job in a male-dominated profession. As a wise colleague later remarked: "Offering to do the job that no one else wants to do can help get your foot in the door." I ended up teaching in three different correctional institutions for nearly a decade, and during those years, I learned quite a bit about motivating students to write.

Being a Female in a Male Prison

Marion Correctional Institution sat far out of town among small farms in rural Ohio, whose owners often worked as prison guards to fund their dwindling incomes. The sprawling facility, built in 1954, housed 3,000 men in overcrowded dormitory rooms full of bunk beds only two feet apart. Each day, I entered the lobby and stood in line to enter the prison. The sign outside the main gate displayed an intimidating warning: *Anyone entering this facility can be subject to a cavity search.*

The huge metal gates were old, and the bars were covered with layers of paint. First, there was an electric buzzer sound, and the gate mechanically slid open with a loud clang. When the gate slowly closed behind me, the same metallic clang seemed to reverberate through my bones. I entered the barren security room and placed my bag and coat on the conveyor belt. I had been warned that the guards were not in favor of a free college education for inmates, so I was wary of any interaction with them. The first guard checked my possessions manually before sending it through the metal detector. Then, the second guard in the booth behind the glass window told me to walk through the metal detector. Inevitably, the alarm would go off. The mic would click on, and the guard in the booth would order the other guard to check me with the hand-held wand. The wand would slowly pass over me and then beep at my feet. I would have to take off my shoes and walk through the metal detector again. Every day, it was the same routine, sometimes delaying me a good ten minutes or more. I tried every type of shoes I owned to no avail. I finally remarked to the guard that I was sure that my shoes had no metal in them. The guard told me that all shoes have a metal bar inside them. I did not believe him for a second. That summer plastic jelly shoes were popular for children, so I purchased a pair, hoping to catch them at their little game. This time when the alarm sounded, I knew for sure that the guard in the booth was setting off the alarm so he and his friend could hassle me. The guards had no respect for a woman teaching in prison.

After clearing the main gate and security check, I had a long walk down several wide corridors that were covered in layers of thick glossy paint. I went by several offices and the glass-windowed control booth. Usually, I only saw one or two inmates shuffling slowly down the hall in shower shoes and frayed blue uniforms. The inmates from general population always appeared half asleep, and I looked straight ahead without any eye contact. Having a school was an after-thought, created from one of the dorm rooms deep inside the prison. The last hallway led to the large mess hall. I had to traverse diagonally across the large room to reach a door to a staircase that led to the school. I would try to hold my breath for as long as I could, limiting the amount of overpowering stench I would smell: a mixture of industrial floor cleaner, rotting food, and sweat. The huge hall was usually being mopped after breakfast when I entered but was full of seated inmates eating lunch when I left. During the first weeks I was there, the men would erupt in loud cat calls and lewd sounds. With my head down and a strong pace, I navigated through a maze of metal tables with attached swing-out seats bolted to the floor. Only one guard was stationed in a room full of hundreds of noisy inmates. One day as I passed through the center of the room, a large guard suddenly blocked my path. I had my head down and almost ran into him.

The guard remarked, "That's a nice sweater you're wearing." His voice was purposely loud for all to hear, and all the inmates abruptly quieted. I slightly raised my head but did not make eye contact. I stood still and waited for what was to come next.

The guard said, "I liked the tight one that you wore the other day better." While the laughter resounded through the mess hall, I carefully stepped around the guard and quickly walked to the exit.

On the first day I taught in prison I was somewhat afraid. I even wore my running shoes, just in case I needed to make a fast exit. There were two education offices and four classrooms: two for GED prep and two for college courses. My introduction to basic writing was met with stony silence from my new students. My exuberance for making learning interesting must have been somewhat overwhelming. Class was almost over when loud noises came from the room next door. It sounded like an argument, and the noise seemed to travel out into the hallway. I told my students to stay seated and peeked out the classroom door. The GED teacher waved me back into my classroom and said that the guard was coming. At the end of that class, I gathered my books and headed out of the room with my students, never realizing that I had left my rear flanks exposed. As the inmates exited around me, I felt a pinch on my bottom. I realized then that I needed to be the last person out of the door to avoid being grabbed from behind.

After I had taught for a semester, I gained some respect, and the inmates would clue me in on their jargon and institutional realities. That winter I wore my favorite turquoise blue fuzzy knit hat into the cold prison. As class ended Robert quietly told me of my mistake.

"Don't be wearing that hat in here no more."

"Why not?"

"Everybody here wants it and would kill for it."

I thanked him. Real knit hats were a rare commodity in prison. Heat was not turned on no matter the temperature until after Thanksgiving. Two thirds of my students were Black, and most of them wore skull caps "mushfaked" out of underwear. Their handmade hats bore the brand name of the underwear, upside down on the elastic across their foreheads. I made myself laugh one day when I realized I was teaching a bunch of men with underpants on their heads.

In the middle of a term, the school administrator told me that one of my students would not be coming back. William was a quiet, jittery, young Black man who sat in the back of the room, often bouncing one leg or wiping his hands on his pants. He wrote a powerful paragraph about how as a young child his father had taken him to the local sheriff and had William locked up in jail to scare him into behaving. Evidently, William had made plans to attack me as the men exited for lunch. William revealed his plan to a friend who thankfully snitched the plan to the priest who then reported it to the warden. William's life was in danger from one of the gangs in prison. For his safety William wanted to be moved to a maximum-security facility. Harming an employee would have guaranteed a transfer. During my time working at Marion prison, a female social worker was nearly beaten to death in her office. Make no mistake: teaching in prison was dangerous. In our introduction to teaching in prison we were told that *safety was job one*.

I had an hour drive from Columbus to the prison. Most of my route was on a boring, rural state road. I had to take our daughter to a babysitter, so occasionally I would be running late. I got an expensive ticket for speeding and resolved never to let it happen again. As I was pulling up to the huge prison parking lot one cold February, I noticed the flashing lights of a State Highway patrol car behind me. I pulled over immediately and waited for the officer to approach. I was sure that I had not been speeding. I grabbed my license and fished the registration out of the glove box. The officer slowly looked them over and ordered me to get out of the car. He then instructed me to get into the front seat of his cruiser. The wind whipped at my coat from across the empty fields as I walked to his cruiser. I wondered what the hell was going on. The front seat of the cruiser was crowded with a rifle mounted upright to the front of the dash. He turned his radio off and moved a clipboard out of the way. I felt creepy having to sit there and turned my cramped legs toward the door. Finally, the officer asked if I worked in the prison. I replied that I did. He went into a half-hearted spiel about how I should consider applying to be a patrol officer. I only remember looking out the window at the prison and wanting to leave. He said something about not speeding on that road and finally let me go. Several of the dormitory windows faced that road, and all the inmates had a good laugh about me getting pulled over by the state highway patrol.

While finishing my dissertation, I started searching for a job as an assistant professor. That spring there were very few tenure-track openings available to teach writing in central and western Ohio. I could not even get one interview. I spotted an ad for a position at Urbana University, located in a small town between Columbus and Dayton. Urbana had two large prison programs: a men's prison in London and a women's one in Marysville. I was offered a full-time job, but the only catch was that Urbana wanted me to start that summer and I already had to teach courses at Marion prison. Both prisons for men were far apart in opposite directions from home and our second child was still a baby. I managed to get a schedule teaching two days a week in Marion prison and two days a week in London prison. The prisons were an hour and a half apart. I spent one night a week in a motel near to the first prison to shorten my drive and give me time to finish writing my dissertation at night.

Memorable Students

In addition to my composition courses at London Correctional, Urbana assigned me to be the only advisor for about 250 inmates who were all funded by Pell or Veteran grants. I sometimes did advising during the day and then taught a class at night. This also meant that I only had time to teach one summer in the women's prison. I met with each of the men and arranged their schedules. The placement tests indicated that most of the men had to take remedial courses in math, reading, and writing. One man started trembling all over when I told him that he was going to have to take a writing course. I realized then that some of the men were more afraid of their writing teacher than I was of them. Terrance, a tall, slender Black man with an Afro, tried to talk me out of making him take a writing class.

Staring wide-eyed at me Terrance declared, "I heard that the writing teacher is really mean."

I knew that I would be his writing teacher. I gave him my most puzzled look. "Really? I know your teacher personally, and that teacher is a really nice person—and a good teacher. You will enjoy that class. Just wait, and you'll see that I am telling you the truth." I looked forward to seeing Terrance's surprise on the first day of class when he realized that I was his teacher.

Having taught public school for eight years prior, I sometimes referred to teaching men in prison as having no appreciable difference from teaching junior high students: both groups were as likely to break out in a fight as to break out in tears about something. I even put stickers on the inmates' papers for doing good work. They really liked the scratch and sniff stickers—especially the skunk and motor oil ones. On the first day of class one semester, Damon surprised me by sauntering into class a good ten minutes late. Damon was outspoken, short, stocky, Black. He slowly strutted across the front of the classroom, interrupting me and gaining everyone's attention. He continued his dramatic performance by pushing a front row desk out of line and sitting down with his legs fully extended in front of him. I had witnessed rebellious theatrics like this before and calmly waited for him to get settled. A few minutes before the end of class, he stood up and turned to head out the door.

"Excuse me," I stated firmly, "I will tell everyone when class is dismissed."

Damon made eye contact and retorted, "It's pizza day for lunch."

I gave him a strong teacher stare, waited, and he reluctantly sat back down. I looked at the rest of the class, restated what the homework assignment was, and paused before calmly saying, "Class dismissed."

The following semester Damon was the school office clerk. Damon was friendly and dependable. He ran off copies and filed records. Damon always checked the office trash cans for something that he could use. He told me how the men recycled trash by refilling markers and turning Styrofoam packaging into coolers. Damon said that they had an elaborate process for peeling postage stamps off envelopes and removing the cancellation marks in order to use them again. I decided to ask him why he was such a jerk on the first day of class.

"I knew I wasn't going to do well in no writing class, so I decided to get over on you before you had a chance to mess with me."

Damon's philosophy about acting out to protect his ego could explain a lot of adolescent behavior problems in junior high.

Some of the men were excellent writers. One term, two white men who always sat in the very back of the room seemed to be competing with one another for good grades. James wrote an outstanding descriptive paragraph about his lonely thoughts when he entered the exercise yard that won him a ten-dollar prize. I produced a two-page newsletter of student writing for all the university basic writing courses and had students vote for the best piece of writing at the end of the term. James won, and I had the university deposit the prize money into his commissary account. On the last day of class, James asked me to settle an argument and proofread Chris's tattoo. Chris was a biker type with lots of bravado. I declined. Before Chris left the room, he came close to the front of my desk and pulled down his lower lip to reveal his *fuck you* tattoo on the inside of his mouth—and it was indeed spelled correctly. Both Chris and James received A's for the course. A couple of semesters later, I saw James in the hall, and he boasted that he was getting the descriptive essay that he had written for my class published. Even though I sincerely doubted that this was true, I smiled at James and told him to "kite" me and I would send him a pass to show it to me. Low and behold, he showed up months later with his article about growing marijuana published in the *Journal of Psychotropic Drugs*. The journal usually printed medical papers but made an exception because they were so impressed by James's writing. James described in great detail how to collect seeds, plant, cross pollinate, nurture, and harvest marijuana in somewhat erotic detail. I told him that as an assistant professor, I was envious of his getting published in an academic journal.

The Best Writing Assignment

I decided to try an assignment with the inmates that previously was a hit with my junior high students. The assignment combined a comparison essay with a large metaphoric graphic glued onto a cardboard poster. I decided to give this assignment to Devan who was in solitary confinement and would miss the final exam. Devan was a tall, muscular Black man who had scared me pretty badly earlier in the term. Devan had come in early to class and put his books on a desk and left. He did not come back. The room was crowded, and the last student came in and had nowhere to sit. I placed Devan's books on the floor and motioned for the student to sit in the empty desk. Just before the end of class Devan came back in. He towered over the student seated in his desk and demanded to know who had put his books on the floor.

I quickly replied, "I did because we were short a desk." I was sitting on the edge of my teacher's desk.

Devan picked up his books and stepped toward me. "How would you like it if I picked up my books like this and wiped the dirt off of the bottom of my books all over your shirt."

This was not a question. It was a threat. He held his books out in front of me and gestured like he was wiping it across my chest. He didn't touch me, and we stared at each other for a few seconds.

"Okay, you made your point," I mumbled and looked away relieved that he did not touch me.

Part way through the final exam time, the students were all silently engaged in writing a traditional essay in their blue books when Devan opened the classroom door and walked in with his large poster project on a full sheet of red cardboard that I had provided. All the men looked up, and their pencils stopped. A low murmur began building across the room. I had been told that Devan was in solitary for stabbing another inmate over a bag of potato chips. The room felt tense, and I was worried that a fight was about to erupt as some kind of retaliation. Devan was now next to my desk. I decided to buy some time by having Devan explain his project to the class.

Devan faced me and began talking. "I compared inmates to pawns on a chessboard."

I risked a smile and said, "A great metaphor. Go on."

"The only magazine that I could get was a *TV Guide*, so I searched through the whole thing until I could find a couple of white and Black faces that were the same size to put on the top of the pawn. I had to tear the faces out real careful like because they don't 'low no scissors."

I silently looked at the drawing he had made of a pawn behind bars sitting on top of a chessboard.

"It's about how guards use inmates in their game of proving they's got power over us."

I thanked him and placed the project on the corner of my desk. Devan turned and slid silently out of the door, and the mumbling immediately started again from the students at their desks.

This time I stood up and asked, "What is the problem?"

"We didn't get to do no projects," one inmate seated in the back row grumbled.

"Yeah," another chimed in, "no fair."

Without missing a beat, I said, "Those of you who pass this basic writing course will get to make a poster project next term in Freshman English. So get back to your writing."

With little hesitation the men all turned back to their writing, and I took a long deep breath.

The next term, I went over the assignment, had the men brainstorm topics that came from their lives inside and outside of prison, and gave each student a large sheet of posterboard. I encouraged students to combine their writing into their graphic in some way rather than just stapling it to the corner of the project. Of course, I had not thought about how they would be able to accomplish this task without scissors or art supplies. (Evidently, there were some paints and brushes around from the art class that had been offered a previous term.) I never knew then that inmates had to pay for goods and services like typing from other inmates, with cigarettes as currency. James drew a defunct robot repair factory to explain how inmates are broken and incarcerated without being repaired. Chris wrote about the evils of watching too much TV. He glued his essay onto a cardboard circle and placed it behind a posterboard sheet with a television set on it with a cut out screen. He used a small section of a pencil to join the two so that the wheel could be rotated to view the essay through the television screen. Big Bird, a rotund white man whose last name was *Bird*, used parts of a discarded pull-down window shade fixed inside of a rectangular box. On the front he drew a boom box, and his essay unrolled as he pulled it out of the bottom. Some students made three-dimensional projects for their essays like a pay phone, fuse box, and even huge models of the whole prison complex.

The projects were so impressive that I wanted to show them off to the public. I made an appointment with the warden, whom I had never seen. I blurted out my proposal to use the visit room for an exhibition of the inmates' projects. I knew that the warden alone had the power to grant my request. I sat quietly and waited for the warden to respond in some way. He remained quiet for a long time and finally granted my request to use the room but warned that only people who already had ID badges could enter the visit room. He permitted the cooks to make a cake and provide

Kool-Aid for the event. The men ironed sheets to cover the visit tables where the projects were displayed. The only audience that I could come up with was the other university faculty who had gone through a background check and were willing to attend. I knew that it would be a small number. I appealed to the school administrator. He managed to persuade the warden to let each inmate invite one friend from general population to attend. That afternoon there was a long wait for the few faculty members to go through security. Finally, faculty began walking up and down the aisles, looking at the inmates' projects. I realized that I should have prepared the students to stand by their projects and explain what they had written. The inmates were all standing near to me against the wall, watching the visitors.

Big Bird spoke to me in a hushed voice. "That woman is looking at my project."

"Bird, go over there and tell her what it is about."

"Nah, she can just look at it if she wants."

I could not convince one student to leave the safety of standing against the wall. Later, an inmate from general population who was helping clean up told me that he wanted to take the class.

"I've got a really good idea for a project already."

The inmates were really disappointed that the reporter from the Springfield newspaper did not show. He had warned that he might not be able to come if there were a bigger news story that day. The reporter did manage to come at a later date. However, for him to be able to take a photograph, the inmate in the picture had to have his lawyer sign a release form. The men had nowhere to keep their large projects, so I took them to my campus office. I often showed the projects to teachers around the state when I did workshops about motivating students to write. I should have taken pictures of them all. Regretfully, one winter break the whole roof of the building collapsed into my office and destroyed most of them. Only a few survived.

Through the writing of my inmate students, I learned many things about their experiences and philosophies about life. Occasionally, colleagues would later ask me questions about what it was like teaching in prison. They would joke that the inmates probably had a lot of time of their hands to do their assignments or that I was teaching to a captive audience. Mostly, people wanted their stereotypes about rape and violence confirmed. I wished that these people could have read the inmate students' writing. All students need to write about their lives and their efforts need to be celebrated and appreciated.

One inmate was quoted by the reporter as saying, "Now ... I know that I can express myself. Before, I knew what I wanted to say but I didn't know how to say it."

Travels on the Prairie and Other Adventures in Academia

Edith Borchardt

Morris, Minnesota, is a railroad town that was founded in 1871 and took its name from the Chief Engineer of the St. Paul and Pacific Railroad, Charles F. Morris. Many decades ago, trains filled with orphans came through this city, where future foster parents waited for them on the station platform. In a social experiment between 1853 and the beginning of the twentieth century, orphaned children from New York City were placed with families on the farms of the Midwest to save them from a life in poverty and perhaps even criminality. These trains stopped in more than 45 states, as well as Canada and Mexico. In Morris, too, these children got off the trains, but that is not the story that I want to tell here. The town's origins with the railroad underline the irony of its unreachability by public transportation in this modern age and present time. Only freight trains rumble through town these days, whistling at predictable intervals, audible especially at night and shaking houses along the railroad tracks. There is no bus connection to the outside world, no limousine for a ride to the airport; there are no vans or taxis for a ride to Alexandria for a shopping trip or hospital stay or visit.

Once upon a time, it used to be different. They say that passenger trains went to Minneapolis several times a day, and in 1985, when I began to teach at the University of Minnesota at Morris, it still was possible to take the bus early in the morning, have lunch on Nicollet Avenue after a three-hour ride, attend a musical at the Orpheum on Hennepin, and return to Morris on the bus at 5:30 p.m. However, this bus connection was terminated suddenly within the first year of my arrival. For a while, different bus lines, like Greyhound and Jackrabbit, stopped once a day in Benson (pop. 3,379), a town twenty miles southeast of Morris (pop. 5,206), leaving early in the morning and returning in the evening. The problem was that one had to get to Benson first to board the bus. There was no bus station, and the stops were moved at random now and then. In the end, the bus to and from Minneapolis stopped at a gas station that had already closed by nine or ten in the evening.

For professors who also had teaching obligations on the Minneapolis campus of the University, who did not always want to commute by car, the cessation of the bus connection was especially problematic. I heard that in a town hall meeting regarding this issue, a professor from Austria expressed the view that public transport was "not a privilege but a right." He was told that family members or relatives could bring him to the bus in Benson. This attitude of the locals bothered me, because I had no family or relatives living close by, as was the case also for colleagues from foreign countries or other states of the USA. At that time, I did not own a car, because my '68 Ford Falcon was totaled in an accident after an NEH Summer Seminar at the University of Washington. An uninsured small truck rear-ended my car in the outermost lane of dense traffic on I-5 and transformed the left fender in the back of the steel frame of my car into the pleats of an accordion. Even if I had owned a car, it would have been impossible to park for several days on the street somewhere until my return to Benson.

Some years later, I dared ask permission from the owner of a bowling alley in Alexandria to leave my newly acquired used Chevrolet Citation for ten days in March in his parking lot. From there, I took the airport limousine to Minneapolis, in order to fly to a conference in Florida and then take a few days of vacation in New Orleans. On my return, I found my car with flat tires behind a pile of dirty snow. A street gang, who had some quarrel with the owner of the bowling alley, had expressed their anger at him by slashing my tires. That I managed to get back to Alexandria at all was due to a chance encounter. Because of construction at the airport, I could not locate the information booth to find out where the limousine for my return trip was parked. As I was wandering around outside of the arrival area, I unexpectedly ran into two colleagues from my campus. I asked them if they were also searching for the limousine stop, and they told me that they had borrowed a car from the University. I asked them for a ride home, if they were willing to take a detour via Alexandria to pick up my car there. When we got there, it turned out that the tires had been slashed. Asked about what to do next, I decided without further ado to ride back to Morris with my colleagues, to report the vandalism to the police in Alexandria from home, to have an officer log the details, and to have my car towed to a repair shop in Morris. A few weeks later, I found out that the police had arrested the culprits, who had to make restitution. They repaid me for the new tires in small amounts dribbling in, for which I created a separate bank account. I also received a letter of apology from at least one of the offenders. He asked for forgiveness, which I granted him, because it happened to be Easter.

Another time, on my way back to Morris a few days into the New Year, I was waiting at the bus depot in Minneapolis to return to Benson. The roads were coated in ice, the temperature sank to minus twenty degrees, and my bus—scheduled to depart at 5:30 p.m.—was delayed. There was no way of knowing when it would arrive under these circumstances. I had arranged with the secretary of my division, who lived nearby in Hancock (pop. 843), to pick me up in Benson at the gas station when I arrived and bring me home. Since I had no idea when the bus would come, I called her from a telephone booth in the bus station (not everyone had cell phones at that time) to ask her not to come to meet me, because I could not expect her to wait for me in her car, perhaps for hours, in those frigid temperatures. There was no café, no bar or restaurant that would have been open after 9 p.m., where she could have gone to stay warm.

The bus arrived two hours late in Minneapolis and on the way out of the city had a flat tire. Changing tires caused even more of a delay on the way to Benson. If I had harbored some hope of finding a telephone somewhere—perhaps in the bar across from the gas station—at that late hour, to tell our Division secretary of my arrival and ask her to pick me up, I now realized on the bus that was moving through the icy darkness on the highway that there would be no possibility of communicating with her, since I wouldn't arrive until midnight. What was I to do? Maybe I could walk to a hotel somewhere in town in spite of the cold and book a room for the night? Where was the local police station? Maybe I could call our secretary from there. Perhaps McDonald's around the corner from the gas station might still be open after all? Then I remembered the old saying, "[Wo-]Man proposes, God disposes." God would find a solution, I thought, and I prayed incessantly and fervently for a rescue during the long ride into the unknown.

When I got off the bus in Benson at the gas station that was closed, I noticed a young girl who wore a burgundy hoodie with MORRIS written on it in golden letters. I asked her if she was driving back to Morris. "Yes," she replied, but she was waiting for a friend from campus who was supposed to be on this bus. It turned out that he was not on board, but she had company after all on her return trip, for which I rewarded her generously. She was a student at the University and lived practically around the corner from me. Later we found out that her friend had gone to Alexandria instead of Benson, where someone else had picked him up. The students had created a network to help their friends who were stranded in emergency situations and brought them safely home over icy streets in those life-threatening temperatures.

Travels on the Prairie and Other Adventures (Borchardt) 155

The Morris campus is part of the greater University of Minnesota and at the time I taught there was considered "The Pearl on the Prairie" and because of its high academic standards "The Jewel in the Crown" within the larger system. The central administration was in Minneapolis, and obtaining tenure was a two-tiered process: after the initial decision by the Tenure Committee and colleagues of higher rank within the Division, internal and external evaluations were performed by committees at what was called Level I (on the home campus) and Level II (in Minneapolis). In effect, tenure was granted on both campuses, and if my campus of close to 2,000 students had been closed, as was threatened several times, I would have had to be relocated to the main campus. When I was called for my interview in Morris in my last year of a temporary position at Lewis and Clark College in Portland, I had never heard of this Public Liberal Arts College out on the Minnesota prairie before and had to look it up in Barron's Guide. What I read there about the divisional structure of the campus and the caliber of the students impressed me very much, and I was happy to accept an appointment there, notwithstanding its remote location. Only after I had made an oral commitment to this campus did I receive an invitation for an interview for a position in the German department in Minneapolis, which I declined, since I had already given my word to accept the tenure-track job in Morris, though I had not yet signed the employment contract. I did not do this out of moral obligation, but because I was convinced that Morris was the right place for me. My ideal was to teach undergraduates at a small college and live on the edge of campus. That this college happened to be part of a large university system was a bonus, especially for my research, since we had excellent interlibrary loan connections. At the edge of campus on one side was the local cemetery, and my colleague in German, who gave me a tour of the town the day after I arrived for my interview, jokingly pointed out to me that here I would have "permanent tenure."

The students in Morris did not disappoint. I had been a "Gypsy Scholar," a roving academic for many years at highly ranked private institutions (among them Gustavus Adolphus College in St. Peter, MN, St. Olaf College in Northfield, MN, and Lewis and Clark College in Portland, OR) while researching and writing my dissertation on the early German Romantic writer Heinrich von Kleist. I had experienced many different types of students and could compare the quality of their engagement and intellectual capacity. These rural students, who came from within a radius of 50 miles of our campus, many of them first-generation college students, surprised me with their work ethic, and their interest in and commitment to German: sometimes because of an interest in music and Lieder singing, sometimes because of their relationship with grandparents who spoke

German. They were always prepared for class: they did their homework! In my interview, I had been told that many of them were shy and would not speak in class, but I had no trouble teaching them with communicative methods at the beginning and intermediate levels, and in literature courses, I assigned them oral reports on our texts for each meeting. They happily complied, sending me their work in writing beforehand for corrections, so that their classmates heard correct German in class. On the intermediate level, they wrote interesting short stories and even poetry that we collected in a tri-lingual journal that I co-edited with colleagues in French and Spanish: *Ideas, Idées, Ideen*. One of these assignments, to write about the most unusual or exotic thing they had ever experienced, revealed a hidden aspect of the campus: there were places that were haunted. I had heard rumors of exorcisms before, but when I received a number of ghost stories for this assignment, I asked the Residence Director, who was my dinner guest with his wife, what he thought about these homework submissions. He confirmed these hauntings and the efforts to exorcise the ghosts, who made their presence known because the college is built partly on Native American burial grounds. Morris was formerly one of the many Indian boarding schools (set up by the Catholic Church under contract with the U.S. government in the late 19th century) that tried to assimilate Native Americans to mainstream American culture. The abuses at these schools in America and Canada have recently been well-documented, mass graves dug up, and the inter-generational trauma recorded. No mass graves have so far been found on the Morris campus, though the search continues: archival records indicate that seven students from the former Industrial School for Indians may be buried in unmarked graves on campus. For many decades, restitution has been made to Native Americans by allowing them to attend the institution tuition-free. That is true for the Minneapolis campus, too. On the Morris campus, several Native American languages are now taught: students can take Anishinaabe and Dakota language courses, and there is a Native American and Indigenous Studies major and minor. There are annual healing ceremonies.

One of my assignments was to direct a German play, a course I inherited from my predecessor, the founder of the German department. This was a daunting project for me, considering that I had no theater background at all, neither acting nor directing and producing, though I loved taking the lead in play-acting as a child with my little friends. I decided to engage students on all levels in my classes as actors, a good number of them as a Chorus of Firemen in *Biedermann und die Brandstifter* [The Firebugs] by Max Frisch. The play involved a number of oil barrels that the arsonists in the play install in Biedermann's attic, creating a potentially volatile situation to which Biedermann is blind. He reads the newspaper and is informed about repeated occurrences of arson all over town, but he refuses to recognize the danger under his own roof when the "Firebugs" infiltrate his home to store flammable materials there. Bringing the oil barrels into the theater space almost cancelled the performance before we even started reading and rehearsing the play, because I was informed by maintenance at the college that installing the barrels in the theater was a fire hazard. (It was reassuring to know that they were on the alert!) We had to wash the oil barrels first before bringing them on the set. Our Black Box Theater is a very intimate space, and I inherited the stage setting of the interior of a two-story house from the play produced there previously: *The Effect of Gamma Rays on Man-in-the-Moon Marigolds*. When I approached some of my colleagues in the Theater Department for advice and help, I was assigned an Assistant Director, a student who served as Technical Director and designed part of the stage as a senior project. His crew also took down the set after the performance. Another student took on the lighting responsibilities. A colleague in Theater granted us access to the costume room, and the Morris Fire Department provided the uniforms for the Firemen Chorus. A friend of mine, a Resident Assistant with theater experience, volunteered to do the make-up. Because of the varying levels of German ability in the group of actors, the performance of the play was script-in-hand, but it was eminently successful because of the cooperative efforts of so many of my colleagues and played to an appreciative audience.

I also inherited a second-floor corner office in Camden Hall from my predecessor. Even though I was there occasionally at midnight, I did not encounter any ghosts. The rustling I heard one night near the window facing north turned out to be a bat curled up in some posters rolled up under the corner table. The next morning, I called maintenance, and someone came with a net to capture the lost creature and bring it back where it belonged: up in the attic on the third floor, where the bats hung out. I wonder if it was the same bat that I had previously found attached to the frame of the double-paned window. That time, someone came with a big leather glove to gently remove it and put it back in the attic. The bats gave the historic building a Gothic feeling, occasionally fluttering through the hall outside my office when the doors on both ends of the corridor were open.

My two colleagues in German were very supportive and gave me freedom in teaching my courses. We shared the same text for the three sections of Beginning German, but we did not impose our individual methods on each other and loosely coordinated the testing of our students. Whenever I said ahead of the annual tenure review, "If I get tenure…," they would correct me: "When you get tenure…." We worked well together for the benefit of our students and our German program. When the language requirement was abandoned for several years, German attracted more students than ever who decided to major in the field, usually in combination with another subject area. Many of them went on to prestigious graduate schools.

Some colleagues who had found the campus less welcoming when they arrived decided to dedicate Tuesday evenings to socializing with colleagues from across campus by holding potluck dinners, providing good company and stimulating conversations, creating collegiality and good friendships. I had never experienced anything like this at other institutions and felt a great sense of acceptance and inclusion. Everyone was invited to these "Fat Tuesdays," and the food often was extraordinary, especially when colleagues from other cultures like China and Turkey contributed to the cornucopia of offerings. During orientation, I met some colleagues, not all of them faculty, who would become very good friends. We got together to share dinner and play Trivial Pursuit occasionally, sometimes until dawn. Once this was followed by breakfast at a local café.

Collegiality across disciplines also extended to invitations to lecture on campus. The Theater program invited me to give a presentation on Brecht's Epic Theater after a performance of *Mother Courage*. A colleague in French repeatedly asked me to give demonstrations of "Superlearning" in her methodology class. A colleague in Spanish now and then hosted a meeting of FLARR (Foreign Language Association of the Red River) on our campus, where I gave several lectures, including one on Hochhuth's documentary drama, *Der Stellvertreter [The Deputy]*. There was also a series of Thursday Afternoon Faculty Seminars. In mine, I recreated the spirit of Viennese coffee-house culture around 1900 with posters by Klimt and music by Schoenberg in a talk on "Turn-of-the-Century Vienna: From Artificiality to Authenticity," tracing the development of art from realism to modernism, followed by a social gathering and discussion over coffee and cake (*Torten* baked by myself and some of my students), dinner at a local restaurant after that. Sometimes I went to regional Foreign Language conferences, sharing a ride with colleagues in Spanish. On the national level, I gave presentations annually at meetings of the International Association for the Fantastic in the Arts. The Early German Romantics, like Novalis, were precursors of modern Sci-Fi writers, telling fairy tales dealing with scientific discoveries of his time in the guise of myth. Sometimes my presentations were printed in the *Proceedings* of the Conference with Greenwood Press, sometimes they appeared in the *Journal for the Fantastic in the Arts*.

During my interview in Morris, I was asked if I would be willing to take students abroad, but that did not happen until the decade before I retired. One of my colleagues in German was happy to take student groups to Kassel for a quarter and later a semester every other year. Our students bonded abroad and returned greatly motivated to continue their German major. After this colleague retired, our German students studied abroad individually through programs offered at the Minneapolis campus. When an opportunity opened up to offer a May session course at the Brunnenburg in the South Tyrol in Northern Italy, a new colleague in German and I developed a four-week course dealing with the Austro-Hungarian Empire that was open to students from all disciplines across campus. It consisted of a four-year rotation between Vienna, Prague, Budapest, and Kracow. We always spent two weeks for language and history orientation at the Brunnenburg in Italy, followed by two weeks of field work with projects for the students in the various cities they visited. Since she had expertise in Slavic languages, my colleague chose to lead the programs in Prague and Kracow. Because of my own history, born in Vienna with relatives there and fond memories of my Hungarian-speaking grandmother in the Burgenland, I chose Vienna and Budapest. In the summer preceding the Hungary trip, I studied Hungarian with a private tutor in Budapest, in order to teach my students the basics of communication in Hungarian during their month abroad. I was trained in grammar and translation, while my TA attended the *Kossuth Lajos Egyetem* in Debrecen and learned Hungarian with an audio-lingual method. During the following academic year, we met once a week in my office to practice our skills before taking the students abroad. (She consequently pursued graduate studies relating to Austria-Hungary and continued to learn Hungarian at Ohio State.)

Looking back at my teaching experiences out on the prairie of Minnesota, I can say that they were adventurous, offering me the opportunity to expand my horizons by challenging me to explore unknown territory like developing new courses, directing a play, and taking students abroad. Standards were high for both students and faculty as part of the University of Minnesota system, and there were great expectations for conferencing and publishing. At times, I attended seven conferences a year, both nationally and internationally. That involved a lot of travel. After the first ten years in Morris and numerous travel dilemmas, I met a professional driver for the Rainbow Rider. It was my colleague from Austria in Social Science, who famously had made City Hall aware of our transportation problems, who connected me with this new service, a public transit system serving west central Minnesota, including Stevens County, where Morris is located. By this time, both the Greyhound and Jackrabbit Bus Lines had suspended service between Minneapolis and Benson. There was a Greyhound station in Alexandria at a café that closed by late afternoon, if it was open at all during the day. On one occasion, my driver was waiting for my arrival there in her car in minus twenty-degree temperatures, and the bus was several hours late. Worried about me, she tried to trace the location of the bus and made inquiries to find out where I was. In the meantime, I was stranded on the bus en route, because some hoses had broken and had to be repaired. There was no heat on the bus at this point, but I curled up in my woolen winter coat trying to stay warm. When I finally arrived in Alexandria, my driver declared that from now on, she would take me all the way to the Minneapolis airport and pick me up from there on my return. She did this for twenty years, making it possible for me to travel to conferences and present papers on a regular basis without having to worry about the lack of a shuttle connection. Unfortunately, a couple of strokes put an end to her driving in recent years, and now there is again no way for me to get from Alexandria to Morris when coming from Minneapolis, except to arrange for rides with younger colleagues who are still teaching. I wonder if, aside from the coronavirus pandemic, the steep decline in the student population on the Morris campus is in part due to these transportation problems. It is also affecting the hiring of new faculty.

As I reflect on my career at the University of Minnesota Morris, I would say that my "honeymoon" of blissful cooperation and collegiality on campus lasted about 10 years while there was some continuity within the administration: as long as the Academic Dean and the Chair of my Division who hired me remained the same. With a number of new chancellors, the winds of change arrived on campus, and cooperation became competition, disciplines were pitted against each other fighting for resources and staffing. Financial exigencies did not help the situation. In German, retirees who had tenure were not replaced and the funding for the tenure-track positions was allotted elsewhere. When a new Academic Dean asked me to reduce the German major to a minor, I presented her instead with my proposal for a German Studies major, which was approved on all levels of administration on my campus (including the Campus Assembly consisting of faculty, staff, and student representatives), and by the central administration in Minneapolis, including the Board of Regents. My legacy to this campus when I retired in 2011 was this German Studies program with seven areas of concentration, which involved numerous German speaking faculty from other disciplines instead of the former three in German only. After my retirement, it lasted another 10 years and now has been reduced to two beginning German sections taught by a newly hired part-time faculty member via distance learning from Minneapolis, but all that is another story for another time.

The Not So Good Old Days?
Happy in Hindsight

Eugene Stelzig

When I earned my Ph.D. at Harvard in 1972, I had been eagerly riding a wave of academic successes for a decade, having attended the University of Pennsylvania on a full scholarship, being elected to Phi Beta Kappa as a junior, and winning a Woodrow Wilson fellowship as well as a Thouron British-American exchange fellowship to study at Cambridge University. I chose the latter, and after two years at King's College, I applied to Harvard, and was awarded a graduate fellowship in the English Department that fully covered my four years en route to the Ph.D. I expected to be able to get a tenure-track appointment in a major university, but when I went on the academic job market in the fall of 1971, I was shocked to encounter the first—but far from last!—major decline in entry-level positions. The Harvard English Department had not yet caught on to this development, and the job advisor was still telling those of us preparing our dossiers to apply to only the top schools we were interested in. My dream of obtaining a position in a leading university, one with a small teaching load, and with courses in my specialty—British Romanticism—where I could devote a significant amount of my time to research and publication, came to nothing. As it turns out, I got only two job offers: a non-tenure-track one in a Humanities program at Michigan State, and a tenure-track one in rural Western New York at one of the 12 SUNY Colleges, some thirty miles south of Rochester. I accepted the latter, and in the long hindsight of more than a half century later, I was even lucky to end up with a tenure-track position in my field, given that some of my fellow graduate student job candidates did not even get an offer—and one ended up taking a job in a community college.

Early in the fall of my first SUNY Geneseo semester, I did get a telephone call from the English Department Chair at the University of

Cincinnati, inviting me to a campus interview. The previous December I had an interview with that university at the MLA convention for a tenure-track English Romanticism position. As it turned out the position had not been filled, and the Chair called me to let me know that the search had been reopened, and that the committee had selected me for a campus visit. I declined that invitation, because I thought it would be unethical and highly disloyal for me to seek a position at another institution when I was just weeks into my new position at Geneseo. Of course, I've often wondered how that road not taken would have turned out had I accepted the invitation and gone on that campus visit.

As a graduate student, I had very limited teaching experience, consisting of being "section man" in two undergraduate courses. This involved doing all the grading for my assigned section of the large lecture course, as well as conducting one meeting a week with the class. I ended up spending the better part of the week preparing for this one-hour class, and so when I discovered that my teaching load at Geneseo would be four courses per semester, I didn't know how I would be able to handle such a demanding assignment. My Department Chair did give me a break for the first semester, by having me only do two preparations (two sections each of two lower-level courses, Intro to Literature and Major British Authors). At Harvard, we teaching assistants were thrown into the classroom without any pedagogical training, and so I really struggled at Geneseo with my demanding load (with about thirty students in each class), in part because I would write out my lectures, leaving little time for class discussion and making for a rather rigid performance on my part. For the first several years, I also tended to be vastly overprepared, which can be as much of a problem as being underprepared. It took me a long time to be as open to the students as I was knowledgeable about the authors and texts I was teaching, but after some trying greenhorn years, I did manage to become a seasoned and successful teacher of a large cohort of undergraduates, both English majors and non-majors. After my stressful and somewhat amateur beginnings in the undergraduate classroom, I earned the SUNY Chancellor's Excellence in Teaching Award in 1984, and in 1996 I was named a SUNY Distinguished Teaching Professor by the SUNY Board of Trustees.

Before I turn to the many positive aspects and benefits I experienced in my Geneseo career, let me mention some of the challenges. Chief among these was the heavy teaching and especially the grading load (essay exams and at least two critical papers in all my courses). This was a constant burden—even when, after some years, the departmental load was reduced to three courses a semester. Because I was a popular professor, my classes usually filled up quickly, unlike some of my colleagues, who ended up having consistently small classes—the division of labor in undergraduate teaching can be very unequal, to say the least. Even when I served a four-year term (1997–2001) as English Department Chair, I still taught two courses. Another negative was the meager starting salary, which did not improve much during the first decade or so. And to add insult to injury, when my wife—whom I had met in England when she had come from Holland to study English at a language school for foreign students, and who had worked as a medical secretary at Harvard during my graduate school years—became a student at Geneseo, we did not even get a break on the tuition from the college administration. And when she met some foreign students who had received tuition waivers, and sought a similar status, she was told she was not eligible because SHE was not really a foreign student!

Throughout my career, I often found the frequent committee meetings—both departmental and college-wide ones—mostly a waste of precious time. And if serving on the English Department search committee, which I did many times, at least produced tangible results, it was also extremely time-consuming and labor intensive, especially when we were doing more than one search and when we sometimes had to screen up to a hundred or more applications for each position. When in the second half of my career I was elected to and served several three-year terms on the college-wide Personnel Committee that was charged with reviewing all renewal, tenure, and promotion candidates, having to read through all those bulky personnel files at a very busy time of the academic year without any course release was quite the burden.

Another negative is that the Vice President for Academic Affairs was determined to downsize the English Department. When I started in 1972 it had 34 full-time faculty, and all the untenured faculty were in constant fear of not getting renewed. As it turns out, most of my fellow junior colleagues were either not renewed the first or second time out, or if they were, subsequently not granted tenure. Indeed, I'm only one of a few survivors of those dire days when the campus administration was perceived as our professional executioner. That unfortunate situation changed significantly by the mid-1980s, when the next two college presidents, who were both former English Department chairs, made it a point to establish more collegial relations between the faculty and administration, which had become extremely strained. However, by the time I retired the size of the department had shrunk to almost half of its former size.

I retired from full-time teaching a decade ago but was able to take advantage of a senior faculty phase-out program that allowed me to teach part-time for several more years. I taught my last class in the summer of 2017, and I'm happy to say that in the long hindsight of memory that the advantages of my career at Geneseo largely outweigh the disadvantages discussed above. I enjoyed living in the East, and having grown up in small towns and rural settings, I enjoyed the village of Geneseo, nestled in the Genesee Valley near Letchworth State Park (with its Grand Canyon of the East) and in the scenic landscape of Western New York with its famed Finger Lakes.

The large Department I joined was very collegial, and I almost immediately formed good relationships with both junior and senior faculty—indeed, many of the former soon became good friends. A signal benefit for someone who had little previous teaching experience was the informal exchanges I had between classes in the English Department lounge with colleagues about how our classes were going, and what teaching strategies were most effective. We were willing to share our pedagogic successes as well as failures, often with a wry sense of humor and encouragement as well as commiseration. These exchanges did much to help me to become a better and more confident teacher, as I came to see how colleagues dealt with some of the same pedagogic challenges I was facing daily. Beyond these pedagogic exchanges, there was an active social life, especially for the first half of my years at the college, when most of the faculty lived in or near Geneseo, with parties almost every weekend that my wife and I came to enjoy. Over the years, I also got into playing various sports with colleagues, including handball, tennis, and basketball. I had been a huge basketball fan for many years, but had never actually played, so the regular Saturday morning half-court games with faculty from different departments was something I looked forward to all week as a great stress reliever as I learned to dribble, pass, and shoot—and hear that ineffable sound as the outside shot swished through the basket—or as I made a layup under it.

I think for many of the graduate students in English of my generation, the study of literary texts in the wake of the New Criticism became a kind of substitute for the religion that most of us had abandoned. Thus, teaching could be seen as a kind of sacred ritual, a priestly celebration of the works on our reading list. Professing and championing literature at a public liberal arts college and sharing my knowledge and expertise with students, many of whom were first-generation college students from the surrounding area, gave me a sense of doing public service and even fulfilling a higher calling. Indeed, I got some wry enjoyment when, in the 1980s, the student newspaper's annual satirical issue had a spoof article about me, with my picture prominently displayed, claiming that I had joined an evangelical church ministry. I certainly took a good deal of missionary satisfaction in being able to motivate students in my lower-level courses to go on to become English majors.

One of the main advantages of working at an undergraduate institution is that I got to teach a broad range of courses, from lower-level ones for both majors and non-majors, to upper-level Major Author courses and senior seminars. I assume that had I obtained a position at a research university, I would have been largely confined to teaching courses in my specialization. Early in my Geneseo career I taught Composition courses, as well as the introductory Creative Writing course. The Composition classes were a challenge, since I had never taken such a course myself, having tested out of the requirement in my freshman year in college. Teaching a variety of courses kept me intellectually alive by working both within but also well beyond my graduate school preparation and training. Years earlier, I had acquired a passionate interest in the writings of Hermann Hesse, and at Geneseo I coupled that with a strong interest in D.H. Lawrence—both authors that I saw extending the perspectives and modes of European Romanticism well into the twentieth century. I developed a popular lower-level Major Authors course on these authors that I taught successfully for many years. In the early 1980s Geneseo implemented a four-credit, two-semester course sequence required of all students: Humanities I and Humanities II. The former included works from the Greeks and the Bible up to Shakespeare, the latter from the seventeenth century to the twentieth. I taught Humanities II for three decades and expanded my intellectual and pedagogic horizon by teaching works by (among others) Locke, Swift, de Tocqueville, Marx, and Freud.

Another lower level offering I developed in the 1970s to meet one of our college's core curriculum requirements and that I taught for several years was Season of Youth. This included works from the later eighteenth century well up into the mid-twentieth, drawn from English, French, and American literature (from Rousseau's *Confessions* to Salinger's *Catcher in the Rye*). In the wake of my Ph.D. dissertation on Wordsworth, I had developed a strong interest in the genre of Autobiography, and I created a course on the topic that I taught for decades in various incarnations, from lower-level offerings for both majors and non-majors (from Augustine, Rousseau, Goethe, Frederick Douglass, and Nabokov, to contemporary American bestselling memoirs by Maxine Hong Kingston, Frank McCourt, Mary Karr, and Richard Rodriguez). I also developed senior seminars on Romantic Autobiography (Wordsworth, De Quincey, Mary Robinson) and Modern Autobiography (from Rousseau and Goethe to Nabokov and even Barack Obama). And for decades I regularly taught the required starter course for English majors, Practical Criticism (later renamed The Practice of Criticism). I also taught British Literature II, a required lower-level course for English majors that covered works from the eighteenth to the twentieth century. I was also able to develop and offer upper-level Major Author courses on Wordsworth and Byron, on D.H. Lawrence, and on Goethe and Byron, as well developing and offering a popular upper-level course on the Romantic Hero, with texts from the later eighteenth century to the mid-twentieth century selected from German, French, English, and American Literature. I was fortunate to be able to teach this course, because the upper-level course on British Romanticism that I was hired to teach was offered only in alternate years.

In the wake of having been a teaching assistant in Harvard's large lecture course on Shakespeare, I had developed a strong interest in teaching his plays, and I was lucky to be able to offer at least one—and on rare occasions two—Shakespeare courses every semester. This was because the upper-level Shakespeare course was a requirement for all English majors—and in those days we had close to four hundred majors! The Department also offered a lower-level Shakespeare course open to both majors and non-majors, and because we only had one faculty member who was trained in Early Modern and Shakespeare, I was able to jump into the breach and teach the Bard to my heart's content. I loved it, even though the classes were always large and thus there was a heavy grading burden. In the second half of my years at Geneseo, the College introduced a highly selective Honors Program, and I regularly taught the Critical Reading course that Honors students were required to take. I taught a course on Shakespeare's problem plays several times—on one occasion, I had an outstanding female student who had developed a passion for Shakespeare during her adolescence and who had read all his plays—a distinction I could not quite claim for myself (I'm several plays short of the entirety of the Bardic canon). I was also able to teach the Critical Reading course several times with a focus on three autobiographies (mostly by Augustine, Rousseau, and Goethe—or sometimes Nabokov). Looking back on my four-plus decades of teaching at a public liberal college, I'm struck by the almost dizzying range of courses and topics that I was allowed and managed to teach and that took me far beyond my official academic specialty. I can't imagine having been allowed to teach such a gamut of authors and topics at a research university.

Team teaching was another source of pedagogic pleasure and collaboration that energized and enhanced my performance in the classroom. My first such venture was during my first years at Geneseo, when a junior colleague specializing in the eighteenth century and I collaborated in offering a course, From Neoclassic to Romantic (with special emphasis on the poetry of Pope and Wordsworth). A senior colleague in the Music Department, a specialist on Beethoven, asked me to join him in designing and teaching a course on The Romantic Spirit in Music and Literature, that we successfully offered four times to a large cohort of students in the 1970s. He and I also collaborated once (at the end of that decade) in teaching a one-credit mini-course on the song poetry of Bob Dylan that enrolled well over a hundred eager students. Sometimes certain pungent smoke odors that were clearly not those of cigarettes wafted down to us from the back rows, and so we decided for legal reasons not repeat that venture. I also taught a trial section of Humanities II with colleagues in History and Philosophy by way of preparing for that new core requirement. My most productive and enjoyable team-teaching experience, however, was with the new college president, Christopher Dahl, who had a background as a Victorianist with a Yale Ph.D., and who had served as an English Department chair before moving up in the administrative ranks. Because he missed his interaction with students in the classroom, he sought me out and asked if we could teach the British Romanticism course together, which he had also taught earlier in his career. We collaborated happily some six times over a decade and a half, and developed an easy and informal back-and-forth instructional style that made the classes productive and enjoyable both for us and the students—who also loved having the college president as their professor (and who had his secretary bring tea and coffee for them in this early-morning class).

One of the attractive teaching opportunities of which I was able to take full advantage was Geneseo's well-established overseas summer study program. The English Department had recently formed a connection with New College at Oxford, and I was able to teach Humanities II in a five-week sequence in residence there, which I did on six occasions between 1997 and 2016. And in the very last part of my time at Geneseo, I taught the same summer course twice in China (Beijing and Hong Kong) and finally once (in 2017) in Berlin. This international and multicultural venture, with various side trips, proved exhilarating to both the groups of some twenty Geneseo students and their eager instructor.

Another truly significant benefit of teaching at an undergraduate institution was that it opened opportunities for NEH fellowships targeted for faculty at such institutions. Two eight-week Summer Seminars for College Teachers—one on Modern Literary Criticism at Yale, taught by Geoffrey Hartman in 1977, and one on Modern Autobiography at the University of North Carolina at Chapel Hill, taught by James Olney in 1983—were intellectually stimulating and allowed me to gain new academic perspective and expertise, as did a year-long NEH seminar on European Romanticism (1978–79) at Indiana University, Bloomington, conducted by Henry H.H. Remak. I also benefited from a four-week NEH Institute on Goethe's *Faust* in the summer of 1990 at the University of California, Santa Barbara. And a yearlong NEH fellowship for college teachers (1983–84) allowed me to complete a book on *Hermann Hesse's Fictions of the Self* (1988) that I had been working on for several years. None of these NEH fellowship opportunities would have been available to me had I not been teaching at an undergraduate institution.

When I started my position at Geneseo, I was pleased to discover that I was not required (by my department or the administration) to confine my scholarship to the area of academic expertise for which I had been hired. While I did publish my revised dissertation on Wordsworth and several articles on him on the road to gaining renewals and tenure, I also published articles on Melville and on Henry James, and conducted research on Hesse, all of which counted for my tenure review. As my post-tenure career progressed, I continued to range widely as a scholar-critic, publishing many articles in the (then) newly developing area of Autobiography studies, including articles not only on Hesse, but also on Rousseau and Goethe. I also worked steadily on a research and writing project that culminated in the publication of my book *The Romantic Subject in Autobiography: Rousseau and Goethe* (2000). Looking back on my academic career, it gives me considerable satisfaction that although I was not able to gain a position in a major research university after earning my Ph.D., I ended up publishing more—and on a wider range of topics and authors—than many of my peers in such prestigious academic settings, and all that despite a consistently heavy teaching load. "Exile at Small-Time U" did not ultimately prevent me from being productive in both teaching and scholarship.

Although in my retirement I now jokingly refer to myself as an Extinguished Teaching Professor, I take both great satisfaction and pride in my busy career at a public liberal arts college and the many students—or generations of students—I taught from 1972 to 2017. I still fondly remember some of them from my very first and anxiety-ridden semester, to those of my later years who stood out for some reason or another. I'm delighted that so many of those for whom I wrote letters of recommendation to graduate, law, and medical schools went on to successful careers. I have kept in touch with a number of them over the years, and I take special pride in the ones who went on to earn a Ph.D.—the most recent one being a brilliant student from an ordinary western New York family on whose letter of recommendation for Harvard I wrote that he was best student I had ever taught. He went on to gain admission to the graduate program with full fellowship support and recently completed his Ph.D. under the direction of a leading Renaissance scholar. He is currently applying for academic positions, but the bad job market is giving him second thoughts about an academic career. He shared with me that "family considerations are making all but the most desirable positions untenable. That is, I'm not going to consider any of the visiting or one- to two-year positions, or the ones in places where we wouldn't want to live, or the very demanding and low-paying non-tenure-track ones when our current situation makes for a significantly better quality of life. And since those few positions are also the most competitive, I am not expecting much this year."

This is yet another example, after more than half a century after I entered the academic job market during its first major downturn, that the situation is even worse now and some of the most qualified Ph.D. candidates in English Studies may decide not to enter the profession.

About the Contributors

Evren **Altinkas** is an adjunct professor at the University of Guelph. He obtained his doctoral degree from Dokuz Eylul University in 2011. His research focuses on the history and politics of the Middle East, Turkish history, and intellectual history. He received the Chevening Scholarship in 1999–2000 and was a MESA Global Academy Fellow in 2020–2021 and 2021–2022. Altinkas is an editor at H-TURK and has published several academic articles and book chapters.

Kathryn D. **Blanchard** is a judicial secretary at the Minnesota Tax Court in St. Paul. She earned her Ph.D. in religious studies from Duke University and is formerly the Charles A. Dana Professor of Religious Studies at Alma College. She is author of *The Protestant Ethic or the Spirit of Capitalism: Christians, Freedom, and the Free Market* (Wipf and Stock, 2010) and co-editor of *Lady Parts: Biblical Women and the Vagina Monologues* (Wipf and Stock, 2013).

Matthew **Boedy** is a professor of rhetoric and composition at the University of North Georgia. He earned a Ph.D. in rhetoric and composition from the University of South Carolina. He is president of the Georgia conference of the American Association of University Professors. He is the author of *Speaking of Evil: Rhetoric and the Responsibility to and for Language* (Rowman & Littlefield, 2018). His book about the rise of Christian Nationalism will be published in 2025.

Edith **Borchardt**, professor emerita from the University of Minnesota at Morris, earned her Ph.D. from the University of California, Berkeley. She taught all levels of German language and literature, German cinema, and Austrian studies, as well as overseas courses in Italy, Austria, and Hungary. The first part of her essay in this volume was originally published in German in TRANS-LIT2 (*Reisen auf der Prärie*, XXIV: 1, 69–72, Spring 2018) and has been translated for this collection.

Camden **Burd** is assistant professor of history at Clemson University, where he researches and writes on topics related to American environmental history. He earned a Ph.D. in history from the University of Rochester. He is the author of *The Roots of Flower City: Horticulture, Empire, and the Remaking of Rochester, New York* (Cornell UP, 2024). His work has also appeared in *Agricultural History*, *The Michigan Historical Review*, and several edited collections.

Derek Charles **Catsam** is a professor of history and the Kathlyn Cosper Dunagan Professor in the Humanities at the University of Texas–Permian Basin, and is a senior research associate at Rhodes University in Makhanda, South Africa. He is editor of *Struggle for a Free South Africa: Campus Anti-Apartheid Movements in Africa and the United States, 1960–1994* (Routledge, 2024) and author of *Don't Stick to Sports: The American Athlete's Fight Against Injustice* (Rowman & Littlefield, 2023).

Wayne Wisher **Combs** is an associate professor at a community college in the upper South. He earned his Ph.D. from a state university in the western United States. He is author of various articles on religion, history, and politics, published in various journals, and the author of a book on early Christianity. His most recent research is on the post–Civil War Reconstruction era.

G. Thomas **Couser** taught at Connecticut College from 1976 to 1982, then at Hofstra University, where he founded the Disability Studies Program, until his retirement in 2011. He then became a lecturer in the Narrative Medicine program at Columbia University. His books include *Vulnerable Subjects: Ethics and Life Writing* (Cornell, 2004) and *Memoir: An Introduction* (Oxford, 2012). He has also published personal essays and *Letter to My Father: A Memoir* (Hamilton, 2017).

Chene Richard **Heady** is a professor of English at Longwood University in Farmville, Virginia. He has taught at several different colleges (and one middle school) in the Midwestern and Southern states. In addition to essays for the general and academic markets, he is author of *Worlds of Common Prayer: Liturgical Time and Poetic Re-Enchantment, 1827–1935* (Fairleigh Dickinson UP, 2019) and *Numbering My Days: How the Liturgical Calendar Rearranged My Life* (Ignatius Press, 2016).

Douglas **Higbee** is a professor of English and the John and Mary P. Grew Chair in American Studies at the University of South Carolina, Aiken. He earned his Ph.D. from the University of California, Irvine. He is the former editor of *The Oswald Review*, a co-author of *In Their Own Words: Augusta and Aiken Veterans Remember World War II* (Augusta Historical Society, 2017) and editor of *Military Culture and Education* (Ashgate/Routledge, 2010).

Erin B. **Jensen** is an associate professor of English at Belmont Abbey College in North Carolina, where she teaches courses in communication, rhetoric, and technical writing. She earned her Ph.D. from the University of Utah. She enjoys creating projects that involve students in research and publication opportunities. She is co-author of recent articles on teaching writing and research in *The Sport Journal* and in the MLA essay collection *Teaching Literature in the Online Classroom*.

Suzanne **Kamata** is an associate professor of global education at Naruto University of Education in Japan. Her research interests include creative writing, the use of literature in language teaching, gender issues, and disability. In addition to her academic writing, she is the author of several works of fiction and a memoir, including *The Baseball Widow* (Wyatt-MacKenzie, 2022) and *Squeaky Wheels: Travels with My Daughter by Train, Plane, Metro, Tuk-tuk and Wheelchair* (Wyatt-MacKenzie, 2019).

Evan A. **Kutzler** is an associate professor of history at Western Michigan University. He earned his Ph.D. from the University of South Carolina. He has published five book-length projects, including a monograph, *Living by Inches: The Smells, Sounds, Tastes, and Feeling of Captivity in Civil War Prisons* (U of North Carolina

About the Contributors   173

P, 2019). From 2016 to 2023, he taught U.S. and public history at Georgia Southwestern State University in Americus, Georgia.

Nancy **Mack** is a professor emeritus of English at Wright State University and the author of *Engaging Writers with Multigenre Research Projects* and two volumes about teaching grammar with poetry. She has published articles and chapters about teaching memoir, emotional labor, and working-class and first-generation students. Her community service projects include partnerships with the National Endowment for the Arts, the Ohio Arts Council, Dayton Public Television, and the Ohio Department of Education.

Matthew **McKeague** is an associate professor of media and journalism at Commonwealth University of Pennsylvania, Lock Haven. His research examines the connection between media production techniques and humor theory. In the past, he has worked as a film and video game critic, production assistant, comedy writer, and video editor in Los Angeles. His research has been published in *Comedy Studies*, *The European Journal of Humour Research*, and the *Journal of Film and Screen Media*, among others.

Camilo **Peralta** is an associate professor of English at Joliet Junior College. He focuses on science fiction, fantasy, and religion, including the work of Ray Bradbury, J.R.R. Tolkien, and Stephen King. Some of his recent work has appeared in *Mythlore*, *The New Ray Bradbury Review*, and *Symbolism*, and he is the author of *The Wizard of Mecosta: Russell Kirk, Gothic Fiction, and the Moral Imagination* (Vernon Press, 2024).

Eugene **Stelzig** earned his Ph.D. from Harvard in 1972 and is a Distinguished Teaching Professor of English Emeritus at SUNY Geneseo. In addition to articles on Romanticism and autobiography studies, he has published books on Wordsworth, Hesse, Rousseau and Goethe, and Henry Crabb Robinson, for which he received the Barricelli Book Prize from the International Conference on Romanticism. He has also edited a collection of articles about Romantic autobiography in England and published translations of German poetry.

Elizabeth **Tacke** is assistant professor of English and allied faculty in women's, gender, and sexuality studies at Eastern Illinois University. She is a disability studies scholar who also specializes in cultural rhetorics, life writing studies, prison and disability advocacy, and teacher education. She received her Ph.D. from the University of Michigan and is the author of *An Educator's Guide to the "Myrtle Hardcastle" Mystery Series* (Workman, 2022).

Louis **Young** teaches American government and political theory, among other topics, at a small, rural university in the southeast region of the United States. He earned his Ph.D. in political science from a University of California campus. He has published articles in various journals on ancient political theory, the philosophy of education, modern political theory, radical politics, and current academic trends.

Index

academic freedom 7–8, 28, 37, 82–86, 89, 94–95, 136
adjuncts 4, 22–23, 27–31, 35, 65, 69, 73, 100, 110–111, 116, 133
American Association of University Professors (AAUP) 4, 95–96
Anderson, Alan 43
Andersonville (Civil War prison camp) 40, 42–43
assessment 4–5, 92, 100

Bishop, Amy 142
Brown vs. Board of Education 39
Buckley, William F. 48

Carter, Jimmy 9, 38–41, 45, 127
censorship 82, 85–86, 126
Christians and Christianity 9, 23, 27–28, 40, 131
committees (academic service) 44, 52, 57, 58, 89, 102, 103, 104, 109, 112, 115–119, 132–33, 142, 163; *see also* service (academic)
committees (search or hiring) 16–17, 20, 23–25, 30–31, 40, 50, 66, 76, 78–79, 81, 100, 133, 162
Costello, Elvis 3
course overloads 110, 112, 115
Covid-19 pandemic 6, 30, 45, 51, 54–56, 68, 89–92, 105, 133–34
CRT (Critical Race Theory) 7, 57, 89–91, 93–94

DEI (Diversity, Equity, and Inclusion) 90–91, 93
Dewey, John 3
Dylan, Bob 166

Erdogan, Recep Tayyip 82

faculty senate 45, 89, 91, 94–95
foreign languages 6, 8, 70–71, 78, 104, 158–59

Freud, Sigmund 18
Fulbright grants 97, 106, 108

Gaiman, Neil 54
Gee, Gordon 90
general education 5–8, 17, 35
Gezi Park (Turkey) 10, 81–83
GI Bill 3
Ginsburg, Benjamin 4
graduation 5, 98, 99, 120–21, 126, 129
graduation rates 4, 123

Harvard University 6, 161–63, 168
highways (travel) 47–48, 53, 64, 146, 154

Ingram, Rosa Lee 40

Jackson, J. B. 47–48, 53
Japan 10, 70–79

King, Martin Luther, Jr. 39

Lang, James M. 8, 124
Last Chance U 67
Lawrence, D.H. 19, 102, 165
Leesburg Stockade 43–45

Marx, Karl 99
mental health 52, 67, 103, 112, 116, 121, 123
Modern Language Association convention (MLA) 15–16, 141, 162
9/11 29

Obama, Barack 102

Patrick, Dan 93–94
Plato 17–18, 20

Readings, Bill 4
Reagan, Ronald 4, 127
recession (2007–08) 4, 8
Rufo, Christopher 90

Sartre, Jean-Paul 21
service (academic) 52, 94, 107, 112, 115–117, 128, 132, 142; *see also* committees (academic service)
Shakespeare, William 65, 166
shared governance 10, 52, 89–90, 94, 104
strikes (labor) 52, 60, 100
student evaluations 5, 19, 25, 30, 92, 112, 118

tarot 57–58
Thomas, Dylan 19
To Kill a Mockingbird 55
Turkey 10, 80–86

unemployment 79, 83–85
unions 52, 64, 100

Wallace, David Foster 48–49
Walmart 100, 122
The Waste Land 21

www.ingramcontent.com/pod-product-compliance
Lightning Source LLC
Chambersburg PA
CBHW032047300426
44117CB00009B/1222